W9-BUB-817

599.32   Costello

The world of the prairie dog.
                          125155

MAYWOOD, ILL. PUBLIC LIBRARY
121 S. 5th Ave.

Hours: Mon.-Fri.
            10:00 A. M.-9:00 P. M.
            Sat. 10:00 A. M.-5:30 P. M.

BRANCH LIBRARY 840 S. 17th Ave.

Hours: Mon.-Fri.
            2:00 P. M.-5:30 P. M.
            Sat. 10:00 A. M.-5:30 P. M.

The World of the Prairie Dog

LIVING WORLD BOOKS

John K. Terres, Editor

The World of the Prairie Dog

Text and Photographs by
David F. Costello

J. B. LIPPINCOTT COMPANY
Philadelphia and New York

Copyright © 1970 by David F. Costello
All rights reserved
First Edition
Printed in the United States of America
Library of Congress Catalog Card No.: 70–110650

To my mother and father,
who loved the things of the prairie

125155

Contents

The World of the Prairie Dog

Meet the Prairie Dog

ONCE THERE WERE billions of prairie dogs. Their numbers alone impressed the early explorers on the Great Plains and in the western mountains. But these sociable rodents, living in villages that sometimes extended for many miles, had other peculiarities that impelled travelers to enter long narratives in their journals describing their first sight of the "barking squirrels" of the West.

Coronado and the members of his expedition in 1541 may have been the first white men to see prairie dogs. The French explorers, Louis and François Vérendrye, encountered them in 1742 in Montana and the Dakotas and gave them the name *petit chien*—little dog. But Lewis and Clark, on their expedition of 1804–1806 from the Mississippi River to the Pacific Ocean, gave them their place in history. They described prairie

Family groups are part of the social organization in prairie dog town.

The prairie dog's tail distinguishes the two broad groups.

dogs in their journals and collected the specimen from which the first scientific description was written.

The Lewis and Clark account tells how members of the party poured five barrels of water into a prairie dog hole without filling it. But they dislodged the owner and were able to examine it closely. The record of the expedition, edited by Elliott Coues, states: "The petits chiens are justly named, as they resemble a small dog in some particulars, though they have also some points of similarity to the squirrel. The head resembles the squirrel in every respect, except that the ear is shorter; the tail is like that of the ground-squirrel; the toe-nails are long, the fur is fine, and the long hair is gray."

It has taken us nearly 150 years to learn some of the facts about the lives of these fascinating mammals—a phase of study that never concerned the early travelers. Zebulon Pike saw them on his journey in 1806–1807 and was the first to describe the prairie dog of Kansas, giving it the Indian name *wishtonwish*. George Ord scientifically described the prairie dog in 1815, calling it the Louisiana marmot, *Arctomys ludovicianus,* because it resembled a small marmot or woodchuck and because it lived in what was then known as the Louisiana Territory. Rafinesque gave it the now-accepted generic name *Cynomys* in 1817, and finally, in 1916, N. Hollister systematically described prairie dogs and divided them into two general classes, black-tailed and white-tailed. But the social behavior of the prairie dog remained obscure until John A. King published his study of their group behavior and population dynamics in 1955.

I am glad I saw prairie dogs living essentially as they must have lived for millennia on the prairie. I saw them in Texas, more than forty years ago, where naturalists believe the population was once nearly 800 million. As a boy, I saw thousands on my uncle's ranch in western Nebraska. Later, I encountered them in all the Great Plains and Rocky Mountain regions of their original territory. And finally, in my grassland research on the plains of eastern Colorado, I studied their relations to cattle grazing and wildlife habitat until the rodent killers exterminated them without permission and destroyed my experiments.

Prairie dogs have lived on the grasslands for thousands of years. Under primitive conditions following the Pleistocene glaciation a balance developed between them and the 60 million bison and 40 million pronghorns that roamed the western plains.* In their ecological effects on grasslands they complemented the large grazing mammals and served as a buffer food supply in times of scarcity for the wolves, coyotes, eagles, and scavenger animals that preyed on the larger animals when biological times were good.

Prairie dog towns and cities were elaborate mixtures of rodents, rabbits, birds, snakes, lizards, insects, and other visitors and squatters that found urban residence profitable on the prairie. Prairie dogs furnished the principal food for the black-footed ferret, now one of the rarest mammals on the North American continent. The crater mounds of the prairie dogs proved observation posts for burrowing owls that nested below the ground. And the labyrinthian burrow systems provided dens, protection from predators, and hibernating space for many other small animals. Weeds that grew in the closely cropped sward between prairie dog mounds were palatable to pronghorns and provided dust wallows for the insect-pestered bison. Always there was activity in dog town.

There are seven subspecies of prairie dogs. All dwell where grasses

*Both the bison and the pronghorn are subjects of other books in the Living World series. A complete list of titles appears in the front of this book. — The Editor.

15

A prairie dog town on the Dakota prairie. The mounds are about fifty feet apart, with lush grass between the burrows.

grow, since they are almost strictly vegetarian, but each occupies a separate habitat, depending on its adaptations to climate, vegetation, and soil for burrow construction. The prairie dogs with white-tipped tails are primarily dwellers in the foothills and mountain parks; those with black tails are inhabitants of grasslands on the plains and semidesert country.

The original home of the black-tailed prairie dog was the mixed prairie that covered a belt east of the Rocky Mountains and extended from southern Canada to Texas and Mexico. No one knows how many prairie dogs lived in this vast domain of the antelope and the bison, but Ernest Thompson Seton estimated there were 5 billion black-tailed prairie dogs during the nineteenth century. One Texas town of 25,000 square miles was believed to contain 400 million animals.

The largest prairie dog town I ever saw covered an area of nearly one thousand acres in eastern Colorado. That was more than thirty years ago. Now, a town of two hundred acres is exceptional. A day spent with binoculars in such a town, however, can reveal how these fascinating animals must have carried on their daily activities for thousands of years on the prairie.

Throughout the warmer months, one may see the waddling adults engaged in building their mounds, feeding near their burrows, chirping warnings, playing or fighting, exchanging kisses, sitting on haunches, responding to neighbors' calls, diving into holes with flickering tails, emerging at the all-clear signal, and nuzzling their young.

Prairie dogs like to sit up to watch while they eat. They hold food in their paws like their relatives, the squirrels.

With continued observation, one may learn to recognize individuals. And ultimately, in the light of what is now known, one may learn to recognize social groups, family territories, town wards, and district boundaries. One may even add to scientific knowledge, since all aspects of prairie dog sociology are not known.

The term "prairie dog" is a misnomer, even though the genus name, *Cynomys,* is derived from the Greek word, *Kynos,* meaning dog. Nor are prairie dogs confined to the prairies; they have been observed at altitudes of 12,500 feet in the Rocky Mountains in Colorado.

The prairie dog is a moderately large rodent of the order Rodentia, which includes rats, mice, woodchucks, beavers, and porcupines,* and the family Sciuridae, to which the chipmunks, woodchucks, fox squirrels, ground squirrels, and flying squirrels also belong. Actually the prairie dog is a large, burrowing ground squirrel, with short legs, long toenails, plump body, and a short tail that seems to be inseparably connected with its voice. The tail jerks every time the prairie dog barks, and it flickers rapidly when danger is near.

These plump, tawny rodents have proportionately shorter tails and bodies and are heavier than their ground-squirrel relatives. They vary in length from 13 to 17 inches. In late summer, when fat, they weigh from 1½ to more than 3 pounds.

Male and female prairie dogs resemble each other. The females have eight to twelve nipples which can be observed at nursing time. As a rule, males are somewhat larger than females.

Prairie dogs show exceptional curiosity about their surroundings and have excellent hearing and eyesight. Their eyes are high on their heads and are almost the only parts of their bodies visible when they watch from their burrows. This watchfulness is essential to their existence, since they are beset by enemies such as coyotes and bobcats and by aerial predators

---

*See *The World of the Woodchuck, The World of the Beaver,* and *The World of the Porcupine* in the Living World series. — The Editor.

Curiosity is one of the outstanding characteristics of prairie dogs. Orange coloring in the eyes permits them to withstand the intense glare of the sun.

such as hawks and eagles. Their community life is organized in areas where grasses and weeds can be cut down to provide an unobstructed view in all directions.

The color pattern is simple, without dark bands or other body marks. The species vary somewhat in color, but in general they are grayish, reddish brown, clear buff, or pale cinnamon. The underparts usually are paler than the backs. Depending on the species, the tail is conspicuously tipped with white or black.

Three kinds of prairie dogs have tails tipped with black: the black-tailed prairie dog of the plains, which once was the most numerous of all the species; the Arizona prairie dog, which has a short black tip on a tail that is slightly longer than the black-tailed variety of the plains (once widely distributed from southeastern Arizona, central New Mexico, southwestern Texas, and adjacent portions of Mexico, it is now rare); and the Mexican prairie dog of southeastern Coahuila and northern San Luis Potosi, Mexico, never studied as extensively as its northern relatives, which resembles the black-tailed species of the Great Plains but has a longer tail with more black on its terminal portion.

19

White-tailed prairie dog. The mound of this species is just a pile of loose soil.

Four kinds of prairie dogs have tails tipped with white; these are mountain- and desert-dwelling species.

The white-tailed prairie dog once existed in large colonies at higher altitudes in Montana, Wyoming, Colorado, and Utah. The habitats varied from sagebrush-covered hillsides to dry mountain meadows and open ponderosa-pine timber stands. Though many have been poisoned, colonies still exist in Colorado and Utah.

Gunnison's prairie dog, another white-tailed variety, lives in mountain parks, meadows, and on the high plateaus of southern Colorado and northern New Mexico. Its communities are loosely organized, and individuals frequently live alone in the manner of ground squirrels.

The Zuni prairie dog, or *glo-un* of the Navajo Indians, is similar to the Gunnison's prairie dog but is more cinnamon in color. Its original range included northwestern New Mexico, northern Arizona, and southwestern Colorado, where they once ranged from the high mountain parks to the vast arid plains and semidesert country, but range and numbers are now greatly reduced.

The Utah prairie dog, now considered to be in danger of extinction, has always been restricted to the mountain valleys of central Utah. The terminal half of the tail is white, and a spot of black appears above the eyes.

Some prairie dogs that dig in lignite in western North Dakota are black because of the coal dust in their burrows. Deep-red prairie dogs, colored by the red soils in Oklahoma, once were described as a different species

Black-tailed prairie dog stained black all over by digging in a coal vein.

White prairie dogs have been found in several locations on the Dakota prairies.

with the name *Cynomys pyrrotrichus*. Occasionally albino prairie dogs are reported.

White prairie dogs have been found in Harding County, South Dakota. I photographed some with black eyes—definitely not pure albinos—at Keith and Dorothy Crew's Prairie Homestead near Interior, South Dakota.

The color of prairie dogs is not greatly changed by the molt which occurs twice each year. The spring molt begins at the head and works back to the tail. The fall molt, which changes the summer fur to winter fur, progresses from tail to head. The tail molts only once each year, in summer, at the conclusion of the change to summer fur. The molts produce no secondary variations between the sexes.

The prairie dog's internal structure is well adapted to its primarily vegetarian life on the prairies, the desert grasslands, and in mountain meadows. Incisors, for example, are large and molars are broad. These teeth aid in clipping and chewing grasses and weeds above ground and in removing obstructing roots during burrow construction.

The abdominal viscera are especially structured for a vegetable diet. The caecum—a reservoir for food materials—is exceptionally large, often as large or larger than the stomach. This digestive equipment, according to estimates of scientists, enables 250 prairie dogs to eat as much forage in a day as a thousand-pound cow.

Prairie dogs are often composed, as one may judge by their actions, postures, and voices. On a tranquil summer afternoon, when no enemies are present, they may flatten themselves like rugs and rest peacefully on their mounds. There is much kissing among friends as they go about the business of grazing, exploration, or mound repair. The young engage in comical games, and occasionally there are fights among the oldsters. Most people who see prairie dogs for the first time are intrigued by their roly-poly appearance, their chirping voices, their habit of sitting straight up, their playfulness, and their mutual cooperation in the face of danger.

The gregarious instinct is especially strong among the young. They

22

The prairie dog's incisors are large.

play together and groom one another. Unlike their parents, they sometimes visit neighboring burrows and spend the night with youngsters belonging to other litters. It is amusing to see from three to seven of them sitting upright on their elevated conelike mounds.

In their natural habitat young prairie dogs at first show little fear of enemies. But soon they learn the meanings of voice signals given by their elders. By mingling freely with other young ones and adults in their local area they rapidly become a part of the social structure.

This early socialization helps them learn the details of their home grounds. At first they are not sure which burrow is their own. If the

23

A large abdomen enables the prairie dog to eat enough to grow fat before winter comes. The paws hanging down indicate composure.

Siesta on the mound. While resting in the sunshine, prairie dogs flatten themselves.

Prairie dog babies. These relatively large rocks have been excavated by the parents.

Young prairie dogs explore to learn the location of other burrows.

This young prairie dog allowed the author to approach within five feet. The sun has baked the rain-soaked soil in the mound.

entrance is suddenly plugged while they are outside they wander help-lessly nearby. But soon they know the locations of other burrows and use them when they are in danger.

By late autumn prairie dog young are nearly as large as their parents. Although they may live for eight to ten years, they do not continue to grow throughout life as do their distant relatives, the porcupines.

Prairie dogs exhibit a social order, or hierarchy, somewhat analogous to that of chickens and cattle. Usually a dominant male in the family group has certain rights. I saw this demonstrated by a pure white prairie dog in North Dakota that sat on the highest place on the mound and had first choice of the most succulent grasses. Also, he apparently had the privilege of wandering farther from the home burrow than did his fel-lows. When danger threatened he maintained watch at the burrow en-trance and was the last to disappear into the ground.

Much of a prairie dog's time is occupied by sitting upright to see the approach of danger or to detect invasion of its home territory by prairie dogs from other parts of the town. They show special interest in moving

26

objects, either on the ground or in the air. But inanimate objects foreign to their territory are also investigated with due caution. I have seen them investigate tin cans, a piece of newspaper, and even my camera case, left near burrows while I was taking photographs in another part of the town.

Young prairie dogs in particular are not disturbed by activity that occurs continuously in one place in the town. Recently, while my wife and I spent several hours excavating a burrow, half a dozen youngsters sat within fifty feet and watched us dig.

The playfulness of young prairie dogs has been described many times. They tumble all over one another in their exuberance. When they learn to give the territorial call, which means that all is serene, their efforts may cause them to lose their balance and fall over backwards. Even when they become young adults they still retain some of their urge to play.

Prairie dogs make interesting pets. If caught when young they remain tame even when they are seven or eight years old. They can be taught to follow their owners from place to place and to eat seeds and other food from their hands. In captivity they lose some of their wariness and may remain silent much of the time in the absence of sensory stimuli that affect behavior in a prairie dog town.

Group living in nature undoubtedly contributes to the intricate social behavior of prairie dogs. In a well-organized town, prairie dogs always seem to be aware of the presence and activities of their neighbors. A thousand eyes watch for enemies. And the warning bark signifies by its frequency and intensity the nearness of danger.

The individuals in a local territory know one another and maintain their familiarity by kissing, grooming, mock fighting, and playing. Their

Neck rubbing, kissing, and grooming are part of prairie dog family life.

territory is defended against intruders from other parts of the town. In time of extreme danger, however, any burrow is available for escape.

Cooperation in a prairie dog town in the presence of enemies is demonstrated in various other ways. If a hawk or eagle is sighted, the vocal message is so urgent that every animal dashes to its burrow and disappears. Whereas the town was the scene of multitudinous activities and sociable yips and feeding calls a moment before, it now is a silent landscape devoid of movement or sound. When the danger no longer is apparent, the all-clear signal brings activity back to normal in the town.

When a man walks through a town he creates a circle of barking prairie dogs. At one to two hundred yards ahead, the inhabitants scurry to their mounds and with a final flickering of tails disappear into their burrows. Prairie dogs far to the right and left continue the alarm from the observation posts of their mounds. Those left behind sometimes pop up and continue the protest when the intruder is well on his way.

Prairie dogs react differently when the intruder is a coyote or acts like one. E. W. Nelson reported that he once stalked an antelope by creeping flat on the ground through a prairie dog town. The prairie dogs were excited as much by curiosity as by alarm. He wrote: "As I approached one mound after another the owners would become almost hysterical in their excitement and would sit first on all fours and then stand up at full height on their hind feet, the tail all the time vibrating as though worked by some mechanism, while the barking continued at the intruder as rapidly and explosively as possible." Not until he came within six or eight feet did the prairie dogs dive into their burrows.

Large grazing animals such as pronghorns and cattle do not greatly disturb prairie dogs. I have seen prairie dogs continue to feed or travel from one burrow to another while pronghorns walk through their towns, but they protest vigorously when bison throw dirt and wallow on the bare earthen mounds. (Visitors in Custer State Park in South Dakota and in the Theodore Roosevelt National Memorial Park in North Dakota can see bison, pronghorns, and prairie dogs together, but not in the fantastic

An escape hole. This burrow was connected with an entrance and mound about thirty feet away.

numbers seen by the explorers who crossed the Great Plains.)

In the thousands of years that prairie dogs have lived on the western prairies and mountain slopes and meadows, they have had ample time to develop their unique social organizations and devices for successful living. Outstanding among these devices is the prairie dog's home. Home is a tunnel that descends at an angle, or plunges straight down for four to ten feet or more, and then slants upward or wanders off horizontally for ten to eighty feet. Usually the completed tunnel slants upward to an escape hole through which the prairie dog can burst when pursued by enemies from within. This escape hatch usually is unmarked by any mound of earth or other evidence of its location. No wonder the prairie

This entrance tunnel slants downward at an angle of about 35 degrees.

A cautious search for danger.

dog prefers deep soils for digging rather than the rocky areas that are used for dens by its near relatives, the marmot and the chipmunk.

The burrow may include side tunnels, rest rooms, listening posts, and branches where loose earth and other debris is stored. From the bottom of the angled or vertical entrance the burrow commonly slants upward and may be only a foot or two below the ground surface. Enlargement of the tunnel at this point forms an air trap and prevents flooding the prairie dog from its home. Many a man who has poured water into a prairie dog hole has learned the effectiveness of this design. (Attempts to drown out prairie dogs probably led to the myth that prairie dogs dig to water. This legend of the town well, of course, was exploded when well diggers in later years found the nearest water in prairie dog towns to be several hundred feet down.)

Aside from the animals themselves, the most conspicuous evidence of a prairie dog town is the multitude of mounds and earthen fortifications around the burrow entrances. These take various forms and are a protection against flooding when violent cloudbursts occur. And always they serve as lookout points for the detection of enemies and as signal towers for the prairie dog community.

Daily life in the prairie dog town always begins on the mounds. At sunrise, fat sentinels cautiously look over their crater rims and then emerge to sit in observation. From here alarm calls, all-clear signals, and community chatter keep all inhabitants informed of the doings in prairie dog town. From sunrise to midmorning and from midafternoon until evening the activities of eating, playing, mound building, dashing for cover, or taking sunshine siestas are never completely detached from the mound and the sanctuary of the burrow.

Not all prairie dogs are dormant in winter. In higher mountain country where deep snow persists for many months the animals do go into winter sleep. But the black-tailed prairie dogs of the Great Plains may be seen on bright cold days in midwinter. Various observers have noted the paths of Zuni prairie dogs leading to burrow entrances beneath the snow in late March. East of the Snowy Range in Wyoming, I used to watch the white-tailed prairie dogs moving about their prairie range on the high Laramie Plains in early February.

Black-tailed prairie dogs start breeding in late February in eastern Colorado. White-tailed prairie dogs breed in late March in the mountain meadows in Colorado. The young appear above ground from early May to early June. From this time on through spring and summer the greatest activity in the yearly cycle occurs.

Seasonal changes in plant life cause variations in feeding and accumulation of fat. Communal life reaches its full development as the young grow into adults. When the youngsters become independent of their parents, either may move to new territory. Finally, autumn arrives and with diminishing food supplies the colony members begin their gradual retreat to the underground world they will occupy until the coming of another spring.

Early evening in prairie dog town. All the inhabitants sit on their mounds for a last look at the sun.

Spring

SPRING COMES EARLY for black-tailed prairie dogs. Even when snow lies on the ground, on mild days in the Great Plains and in the semidesert country, a few animals make daily appearances. As early as January or February, pre-breeding activity is indicated by increased contacts between animals that leave their burrows in explorations about the town.

But spring on the far western prairies is a capricious thing. Snowstorms and high winds reduce prairie dog activity, and the animals may remain underground for days at a time. They do not come up regularly until the wheat grasses are two or three inches high, and buffalo grass and blue grama have begun to change the landscape into a sward of endless green.

A black-tailed prairie dog in early spring.

Rubbing noses is common among friends.

Spring

Spring comes late for the white-tailed prairie dogs in the mountain valleys and parks. Before they were poisoned and decimated by plague in southern Colorado I used to see them in colonies of hundreds along Upper Cochetopa Creek and in the ten-thousand-foot-high country north of Gunnison. Snow in parts of this mountain area remains sometimes until July. The prairie dogs have to compress their spring and summer activities into a short season, somewhat in the manner of mountain plants that have adapted themselves to growth, flowering, fruiting, and seed dispersal within a few short weeks.

The early seasonal activities of the mountain-dwelling white-tailed prairie dogs and the plains-dwelling black-tailed subspecies show striking differences. The white-tailed prairie dogs spend little time in social integration. Their clans, which consist mainly of temporary family groups dominated by the mother of a litter, use the short spring and summer season to store fat in their bodies. They do this in preparation for the long snow period that confines them to their underground world.

Jules V. Tileston and Robert R. Lechleitner, in their studies of prairie dog towns in Colorado, have suggested that the lack of social integration among white-tailed prairie dogs allows them more time for feeding, which possibly accounts for their rapid weight gains. This undoubtedly is true. The white-tailed subspecies have much less time for activity above ground. It may be supposed that eating is so important in their lives they never have time to develop a social structure.

Social behavior of black-tailed prairie dogs may thus utilize energy which might otherwise be directed toward accumulating fat. These prairie dogs are also subjected to greater summer heat than their mountain-dwelling relatives and may gain fat more slowly for this reason. At any rate, more information is needed on the nutritive qualities of food and the energy requirements of life in plains and mountain environments before we can explain adequately the differences in social structures and activities of prairie dog subspecies.

Tracks in the snow made by black-tailed prairie dogs indicate that they

35

Male prairie dog leaves for patrol of territory while the female watches for enemies.

do considerable traveling between burrows in January and February. With ameliorating weather conditions, a rhythmical appearance of prairie dog groups occurs during the middle of the day. Food is still scarce, and the animals travel many yards from their burrows to feed. They vigorously clean out old burrows, too.

Colony activity increases with the approach of the mating season. Exploration of territories results in physical contact between males and females. They kiss, and occasional fights arise in which females defend their burrows against males. During the day, while females feed intensely, males defend territorial boundaries, groom themselves, and bask in the sun. At night males frequently retire to their own winter burrows, whereas the females use nesting burrows. During this time there is a large amount of nesting material being carried underground.

As spring advances, activity in well-populated prairie dog towns be-

Spring

comes more animated. A few animals are always exploring, digging up roots, or sitting erect and nibbling grass stems held in their paws. There is much scampering about and sniffing of one another to determine which are friends and neighbors and which are intruders. The *yap-yap-yap* of sentinels begins at the first appearance of an enemy. If there is a real danger, the barking increases in speed and intensity until the callers seem ready to burst with trepidation. In panic the inhabitants dash to their mounds and dive into their burrows with tails flicking a final visual warning. Then all is quiet.

Within minutes or sometimes not for an hour or so, a prairie dog with eyes just above the burrow opening reconnoiters. Then another checks, and another. If the danger is past, the all-clear signal is given. Soon the town is in action again.

The breeding season varies with geography and altitude. On the plains of Kansas it starts around the last week in January. In the Wichita Moun-

The prairie dog's tail is a signaling device and its position indicates the animal's degree of alertness or composure.

tains in Oklahoma, Adam Anthony and D. Foreman captured pregnant females from January 23 to March 28. In eastern Colorado and at Wind Cave, South Dakota, Carl B. Koford observed that black-tailed prairie dogs bred about a month later than those in Oklahoma. On the Laramie Plains, Wyoming, Eugene B. Bakko and Larry N. Brown saw white-tailed prairie dogs mating in late March and early April. Juveniles appeared above ground about mid-June.

Most observers agree that the gestation period for prairie dogs is approximately thirty days. Anthony and Foreman estimated the length of pregnancy to be from twenty-eight to thirty-two days. The average litter size is approximately five, although the number of embryos in dissected females varies from two to ten. Prairie dogs deliver just one litter per year during their life span of four to five years. Some females may not breed at all their first year.

The dates of breeding and the subsequent appearance of young are apparently related to temperature. Tileston and Lechleitner observed that both black-tailed and white-tailed prairie dogs bred when average daily temperatures reached 32 degrees Fahrenheit and that the young appeared above ground when the average daily temperature reached 55 degrees Fahrenheit.

Very few people have ever seen a prairie dog baby immediately after birth. The young do not appear above ground for several weeks, and excavation of burrows to obtain them earlier is such a difficult task that few men have had the will or the energy to attempt it.

In 1927, George Edwin Johnson reported a fascinating series of observations he had made of very young prairie dogs. On April 1, 1925, he found four that had been born the previous day in a laboratory cage. He noted that the mother was solicitous of her young and that she licked them or rubbed them with her mouth. He believed her actions may have been connected with cutting the umbilical cord.

The babies each weighed 15.5 grams (about half an ounce), and their bodies measured 69 mm. (two and three-quarter inches) in length. From

Baby prairie dogs one day old. The mouth parts are better developed than the rest of the body. (George Edwin Johnson, Journal of Mammalogy)

The eyes of thirty-three-day-old prairie dogs (above) are still not open, but at forty-four days of age (below) they can see. (George Edwin Johnson, Journal of Mammalogy)

nose to tip of tail they were 82 mm. (three and a quarter inches) long. Their dark red skins were wrinkled, and between the wrinkles the skin was smooth and shining. Their mouths were better developed than other parts of their bodies, and ears were only slight enlargements under the skin.

The prairie dog babies grew rapidly. Within a week their weight increased by 40 per cent. In thirteen days they were two and one half times heavier than at birth. Fine hairs covered their cheeks, and a few hairs were visible on their bodies. Their eyes bulged under the skin, and ears were visible as folds of skin.

They uttered squeaky sounds by the sixteenth day. Their forelegs were better developed than the rear of the body, and they were able to squirm and roll about. At three weeks of age hair appeared over their bodies, and one animal was able to stand. One week later they could crawl with legs spread sideways from their bodies.

When they were thirty-three to thirty-seven days old, the babies began to open their eyes. At this time they acquired the ability to walk and run about their cage. They barked when disturbed and ate green alfalfa. They started to look like real prairie dogs. Johnson's observations indicated that prairie dog young probably do not appear at the burrow entrance until they are about six weeks old. It also seemed that the young are unable to survive without milk from the mother until they are at least seven weeks old.

Young prairie dogs remain underground for most of the nursing period. Even when they first come out of the burrow, they seldom eat plant life for several days. If they attempt to nurse, however, the mother tends to wean them by moving away. Consequently, they soon learn to forage for themselves.

Life in the early stages above ground has been called a "pup paradise" by John A. King. The young prairie dog plays with other youngsters. All the adults kiss and groom them. When the young attempt to suckle males or females indiscriminately, the females submit, but the

White-tailed prairie dog mother in southwestern Wyoming. Her young have not yet appeared above ground.

These youngsters have been above ground for about three weeks, but they still stay close to the home burrow.

Black-tailed prairie dogs about ten weeks old. At this age they are intensely curious and not greatly frightened by people.

males gently thwart them and groom them instead. The children are rarely punished by biting or kicking.

Prairie dog young are playful creatures and amusing to watch when they congregate above their burrows. The number in a litter can seldom be estimated accurately by counting them on a mound. Soon after they appear above ground, they join with each other in various activities. The adults do not discourage this association, and so there is much scampering of the young between mounds as they grow larger and more sociable.

They learn the meaning of barks and other signals made by adults. At the first indication of danger, they dash into their burrows. This hypersensitivity wears off, however, and they become curious about strange things, displaying differences in personality. Many times I have noted that some youngsters appear to be more venturesome than others. They explore at greater distances from the mound and contact more adults. These bolder ones also start more chasing games than do their associates.

Initiators may be either male or female. While the group is feeding or is engaged in other activities, the playful one starts to creep toward an unwary youngster and then pounces upon the unsuspecting victim. The encounter may end in a wrestling match or in a game of tag in which the pursued individual is not touched but suddenly becomes the pursuer.

Young prairie dogs frequently attempt to play with adults. Generally the adults are friendly. They reciprocate in the play by either tumbling, kissing, grooming, or making mad dashes in and out of burrows. Annoy-

Young prairie dogs kiss, groom, and play together.

ing young are sometimes ignored or repulsed by foot pummeling or by light nips with the teeth.

Wrestling involves a whole group of youngsters and generally occurs near the burrow entrance. The melee results in a blur of action in which individual contestants are indistinguishable. The swirling ball of bodies rolls about and suddenly breaks apart. Then each one interests himself in some activity such as barking, feeding, or basking in the sun.

Pits dug by black-tailed prairie dogs to obtain grass roots for food. Thus in periods of drought they do not go hungry.

Play and other forms of social contact result in the formation of behavior patterns essential to the social organization of the prairie dog town. In the·early weeks of activity the youngsters receive affectionate attention from all adults, even those in adjoining family territories. But as they grow larger, play with friends from different territories sometimes turns into threats or miniature battles. Strangers become antagonistic, and the growing young discover the limits of their own territories. At the same time, they learn the calls that indicate danger or security. As participating members of the town, they cooperate in communicating information to other inhabitants by voice, tail signals, and general behavior.

With the advance of spring the prairie dog young grow and take part in the search for food. From January until March, before the plants of the new season become green, the hunt for grass seeds, cactus plants, and the roots of perennial plants and grasses increases colony activity. Sometimes, many shallow pits are dug in search of blue grama and buffalo grass roots. These pits occasionally pockmark the sod for many yards around the burrows.

Prairie dogs avidly eat cheat grass brome and Russian thistle seedlings, since these are among the earliest green plants to appear on the mixed prairie and in the foothills east of the Rocky Mountains. The Russian thistle seedlings are a good choice, because they contain as much as 23 per cent protein in their early growth stages. Later, when the plants as-

44

The stems of dandelions are eaten first.

sume their globelike forms and become spiny, prairie dogs avoid them.

In late March and early April, new shoots of grasses and forbs—broad-leaved herbs—appear. At this time, prairie dogs increase their foraging. They appear to wander haphazardly in search of food but generally concentrate their efforts in areas where grasses are most abundant. When prairie dogs find green stalks of wallflower or the flowering stems of dandelions, they clip them, sit on their haunches, and hold the plants in their paws, eating the stems and then the flowers.

Black-tailed prairie dogs in Kansas and in the Dakotas give special attention to the little bluestem grasses when they are available. Before the plants are green, the prairie dogs dig pits to obtain the roots. Later they nibble the new green sprouts. Peppergrass is also one of their favorite foods. Stomach analyses of these prairie dogs in early June have shown that peppergrass may make up 50 per cent of their diet.

The proportional amount of each plant in the prairie dog's diet depends partly on the availability of forage types. White-tailed prairie dogs consume sedges and grasses since these are commonly abundant in their habitats. They also browse sagebrush and saltbush when succulent green herbage is scarce.

The spring diet of the prairie dog contains fewer weeds than the summer diet, and the fall diet contains more shrubby species than the summer diet. Thus, the relative food values of different plants and the degree of their selection by prairie dogs shift with the seasons.

Many species of plants growing in prairie dog towns are not eaten. Prairie dogs cut down snow-on-the-mountain, spider-wort, ironweed, and the plains wild indigo and seek green grass as food in preference. Scarlet globe mallow, however, is eaten in quantity when it is present. It is not known if the prairie dogs choose this forb because of its nutritive value, but laboratory analyses have shown that it contains from 18 to 20 per cent protein.

The tall forbs not eaten by prairie dogs are felled and left on the ground by them as a defense measure to increase the visibility of enemies

Prairie dogs communicate with voice signals as they sit on their mounds. The upright tail indicates imminent danger.

and permit better communication among the town inhabitants. I believe that the continued survival of prairie dog towns depends as much on communication as on food and shelter. I have often observed that dog towns vanished in the midst of abundant plant life if predators were able to approach unseen and if the prairie dogs were too few in number to communicate by voice or tail signals.

Several years ago I watched the demise of a prairie dog town west of Grover, Colorado, where predator control crews had poisoned most of the inhabitants. I estimated that less than 10 per cent of the original population remained. The reduced numbers of prairie dogs, not more than one per acre, were unable to clip the veritable jungle of pigweed, sunflowers, and other tall forbs that obscured their mounds in late spring and early summer. Alarm calls between prairie dogs were infrequent. When I walked through the town, individual animals would run to their burrows only after I had made noise in the weeds so they could hear my approach.

Coyotes were numerous in this area. Many of these predators used abandoned badger holes in the town for hiding places. In late August the coyotes had reduced the prairie dog population to two animals. When I visited the town again in mid-September, there was no sound of prairie dog voices.

The voice of the prairie dog has many meanings. The alarm bark is a two-syllable sound. In Kansas, Ronald E. Smith described it as *tic-uhl, tic-uhl, tic-uhl,* the first syllable having a higher pitch and shorter duration than the second. The second syllable always sounds to me as if the prairie dog were drawing in a wheezy breath after giving a *chirk* with an outgoing breath. At a distance, only the *chirk* is audible.

Smith wrote, "The frequency and intensity of this bark is greatest during the first two or three minutes in which it is given; thereafter the frequency slows to around forty barks per minute (this varies considerably) and may continue for as long as an hour and a half. On hearing this bark, all prairie dogs in the immediate vicinity sit up and look around." If the danger appears to be real, they run to their mounds and join in the alarm.

By walking very slowly toward a mound I have found that a prairie dog will frequently stop barking and immediately lie with its belly over the burrow entrance. The tail will flicker periodically or jerk if the prairie dog barks. As one approaches, the prairie dog submerges itself in its hole until all that is visible are the eyes and the tail. By standing perfectly still I have watched them maintain this position for as long as twenty minutes at a time. They rarely emerge even a fraction of an inch; instead, they finally lose patience and disappear into the earth.

The eagle or hawk warning call is much more urgent than the alarm call and causes an instant dash for the burrows. The two notes of the call are uttered at a high pitch and are easily distinguished from all other calls. Badgers will prompt these calls, as well as soaring birds. Hawks sit-

The prairie dog sinks lower and lower into his burrow entrance as an enemy approaches.

ting on the ground cause alarm, but magpies, meadow larks, sparrows, buntings, longspurs, and birds of similar size go practically unnoticed.

John A. King recognized ten different utterances or calls in the language of black-tailed prairie dogs: warning bark, hawk warning, defense bark, muffled bark, territorial call, disputing *churr*, chuckle, fear scream, fighting snarl, and tooth chattering. This classification is based primarily on detailed studies made in Shirttail Canyon in Wind Cave National Park, South Dakota.

The warning bark gives notice of possible danger and may be elicited from prairie dogs by the approach of a bison, cow, coyote, human being, or even the presence of an unnatural object such as an automobile or a piece of paper. It alerts all prairie dogs in the vicinity. Some animals may run to their mounds, sit erect, and take up the call. Others may sit up momentarily and then resume their feeding or other activity of the moment. Ronald E. Smith noted that a few prairie dogs seem to bark at everything,

49

The eagle is one of the most efficient predators. All dogs dash for cover when an eagle appears. (Colorado Game, Fish and Parks Department)

Telephoto shot of prairie dog ready to give the alarm signal for all to submerge.

The territorial or all clear call. This action is difficult to photograph, since it lasts less than one second and one never knows when the call will be made.

including horned larks, rabbits, and grasshoppers. One female he observed barked for an hour and a half without stirring her associates from their routine activities.

It is possible that these long-continued calls serve purposes other than warning the entire colony. William Etkin described calls made by social animals to maintain the sense of familiarity between individuals. In specific situations such calls may have many interpretations, and they are frequently contagious among prairie dogs. Whatever the purpose of such lackadaisical chirping may be, I know that it can instantly change to a real alarm call if danger suddenly appears.

The warning bark of the white-tailed prairie dog is a mechanical-sounding *churk* repeated at half-second intervals. The tempo increases as danger approaches. If the rate reaches four or five barks per second, all prairie dogs rush to their burrows.

The warning call of the Zuni prairie dog is shorter and sharper than that of the plains prairie dogs. Theodore H. Scheffer in his ecological studies (1947) stated that it has "a flavor of foreign accent; perhaps only a local dialect but distinctly different, though not akin to the more pro-longed whistle of the burrowing squirrels in general."

The hawk or predator warning call is similar to the general warning bark, but the second syllable maintains the same high pitch as the first. It is given rapidly as the animal scurries to cover. All other prairie dogs heed this call without waiting to see where the danger is.

The defense bark, as King described it, is a high-pitched note uttered at intervals. It is produced when a male from another territory tries to drive a female back into her own territory or when there is an invasion by an adult into a territory where local males are absent. A softer bark, called the muffled bark, results when two females are protecting their nesting territories. It is ignored by other prairie dogs in the vicinity.

One of the most distinctive calls is the territorial call or all-clear signal. This has been variously described by observers, and it is possible that prairie dogs in different localities use dialects. But it is always executed with a movement of the entire body. Young prairie dogs sometimes fall over backwards when giving it.

Carl B. Koford and other observers have noted that the prairie dog may give this call while sitting on its mound or it may rise from its feeding, stand on its hind legs, point its nose and legs skyward, and utter the first syllable, sounding the second note as it drops its head and forelegs or comes down on all fours. The sound has been described as *aeeee-hau*, and as *ee-ko*. Frequently it is taken up by other prairie dogs in the home territory.

The territorial call has various meanings and is uttered sometimes in the absence of any visible stimulus. It may indicate territorial ownership. John A. King wrote that it may be expected after a hawk or eagle has passed and thus is an "all-clear" call.

I have watched and heard black-tailed prairie dogs give this call hour after hour in the badlands of the Little Missouri River in western North Dakota and believe it also denotes a sense of well-being, of serenity in the colony, or even exuberance in the midst of a plentiful food supply.

Prairie dogs grazing in abundant grass seem to give the call more frequently than those grazing on relatively denuded ground.

The white-tailed prairie dog sounds a different all-clear call. Tilleston said it has a musical quality that resembles a yellow-shafted flicker's shrill descending call. The first component is followed by four notes of equal tone, as *chtaa-chaa-chaa-chaa-chaa*. Once it is given, other members of the colony respond with similar calls.

The *churr* or snarl, according to King, is uttered when a prairie dog becomes angry during a dispute. A male pursuing an unreceptive female may cause her to snarl. Pet prairie dogs may snarl when they do not want to be bothered by their owner. Sometimes they *churr* or snarl during a fight and are especially apt to produce a variety of angry sounds when removed from a trap. Tooth chattering is occasionally heard when prairie dogs are disputing. I have also heard them growl and chatter their teeth when I ran close behind and chased them into their burrows.

The fear scream is characteristic of the young. I have listened to this scream when I removed them from a trap or handled them after they were caught with a noose at the end of a fishing line. King described the fear scream as a series of cries sounding somewhat like the crying of a baby.

My wife once heard the fear scream while sitting on a prairie dog mound near Medora, North Dakota. She had been motionless for some fifteen minutes, watching an adult on a mound some thirty feet away, when a youngster suddenly popped out of its burrow between her hand and her body. Apparently completely surprised by her presence, it froze in the entrance and uttered one cry after another for a period of approximately twenty seconds. My wife insisted that the sound was a scream, not a bark, *churr*, or growl.

White-tailed prairie dogs often growl when they are caught in live traps. Upon release they run to their burrows and make a series of soft chuckles rapidly slurred together. I have heard black-tailed prairie dogs make similar sounds and also listened to them make a low-pitched growl

Prairie dogs kissing. They do this when a friend returns to the mound.

like that of a small dog. The meaning of these forms of sounds merits further study.

One of the amusing and apparently very useful forms of communication among prairie dogs is "kissing." This is done mostly between friends, but it has other connotations in prairie dog society; at times it appears to be contagious. Young ones exchange kisses; adults kiss young; and adults kiss adults. White-tailed prairie dogs are less inclined to exchange kisses than are black-tailed prairie dogs.

The kiss is given when two prairie dogs meet while they are engaged in activities within the family territory. The action involves open-mouth contact, usually with heads side by side, and with teeth showing. Sometimes it is the merest touch. At other times it lasts for ten seconds or more. It is followed frequently by grooming or by the animals lying in contact on the mound or on the grass.

When visual identification at a distance is in doubt, two prairie dogs may creep slowly toward each other, exercising great caution. If they are friends, they will kiss. If one is an intruder from another part of the town, it may suddenly be pursued by the local defender. King believed that the open-mouth approach to the kiss is a warning that the prairie dog is ready to fight if proper identification is not established. Affection is not displayed until the kiss is consummated. Then tail wagging, grooming, nibbling at one another's fur, huddling together, or mock fighting show familiarity between the two animals.

In his observations of prairie dogs in Kansas, Ronald E. Smith observed that the first prairie dog that runs to the mound kisses others as they arrive. Young ones sometimes go around kissing every prairie dog they see. If adults advance and do not kiss, but snarl instead, both may crouch low to the ground. "Then the first one turns around showing the three anal glands, which the other prairie dog smells. Then the position is reversed and the first prairie dog smells the other prairie dog's anal glands. After all this the two prairie dogs wander off to feed."

Kissing, as well as other forms of contact, occurs in prairie dog town since the home range and daily travel generally is limited to an area of an acre or two. Within that territory, however, a multitude of visits are made and a surprising amount of travel is accomplished by individual animals.

Within their home territory, King made crude measurements of the daily distances traveled by black-tailed prairie dogs in the Black Hills of South Dakota. He found that most individuals traveled less than a mile each day. Estimated travel in a fourteen-hour day varied from 3,200 feet to 14,112 feet. The male prairie dog that may have traveled nearly three miles in one day had driven an intruder from his territory and apparently felt it necessary to patrol against further invasion.

Many factors influence the movements of prairie dogs within their home ranges. A pet prairie dog I knew in Colorado was content to feed in lush grass without going more than fifty feet from his cage. On the other hand, I observed prairie dogs traveling more than three hundred feet across a virtually denuded area around their burrows to feed at the borders of tall prairie vegetation in eastern Montana. In one town of nearly two hundred acres I noted much running of animals along a high ridge where they were skylined for several minutes at a time. On investigation I found that they were traveling from their burrows on a bare south slope to a succulent stand of blue grama and western wheat grass on a moist northern slope.

A prairie dog may walk as much as three miles in one day while on patrol.

Many years ago, when the white-tailed prairie dogs were still abundant in Colorado, I used to watch them moving over the sparsely vegetated slopes among the juniper trees north of Salida. They were also numerous on the sandy flats west of the Sangre de Cristo Mountains. Eventually they were poisoned and the colonies almost totally destroyed by sylvatic plague. But, as I remember, they traveled greater distances than the black-tailed prairie dogs on the plains east of the Rocky Mountains. I believe they did this on account of the paucity of nutritious grass, which grew only in widely scattered tufts. Perhaps, also, their loosely developed social structure and lack of definite territorial boundaries allowed more flexibility of movement.

56

Summer

SUMMER is the most important part of the year in prairie dog land. Many of the grasses and forbs are flowering, and their succulent herbage provides nutritious food for the fattening period that ends in early autumn. The long warm days of summer provide many hours for grazing and other activities.

Finding food is easy and time is available for burrow construction, weaning of the young, and establishment of new territories. As family ties are broken, the young become more self-sufficient, and older prairie dogs are free to migrate and explore new areas.

Prairie dog eating succulent grass stems.

Summer is also the bountiful period for other animals. Their presence in prairie dog towns enlivens the colony. Burrowing owls, snakes, resident birds, insects, toads, salamanders, and spiders become a part of the community structure, since they intermingle freely with the prairie dogs. Eagles, coyotes, and black-footed ferrets are fierce predators that affect but do not materially reduce the prairie dog population.

Summer is the best time to watch prairie dogs. One can easily observe their eating habits, their friendship for youngsters and neighbors, and their reactions to other wildlife. To enjoy them most, though, one should have some knowledge of the social behavior that makes them unique among all rodents and among other animals that live in societies for mutual cooperation and protection.

A prairie dog community may consist of hundreds or even thousands of individuals. But within this population are many groups which have their own territories with invisible boundaries established by the animals themselves. John A. King has given the name *coterie* to the basic units which are the lowest kind of social organization in prairie dog towns. Groups of coteries have been called tribal territories, wards, or clans by various investigators.

The composition of coteries varies from place to place, even in the same town. An average coterie may consist of an adult male, several adult females, and half a dozen young. King has observed a coterie with as many as thirty-one youngsters and another with no babies at all.

Each coterie member is known to the others. All share the burrows and food resources of their territory. In moments of tranquility and freedom the members kiss and groom. I am always amused when I see them sitting upright and side by side, each with an arm around a companion's back.

The coterie territory is known by both adults and youngsters. The boundary is defended when males from adjoining territories cross the invisible line. Sometimes interlopers and residents fight. I once observed encounters between prairie dogs stained black with coal dust and prairie

White-tailed prairie dog female in northeastern Utah.

dogs of normal color in the Theodore Roosevelt National Memorial Park in western North Dakota. One coterie seemed to be established above a coal seam, while the other was located in a meadow underlain by deep silt loam. When the black group entered the meadow, they were challenged; the disputes occasionally became violent. Scars on the faces of some of the older animals were mute evidence of past hostility between these coteries.

Colony organization is most highly developed among the black-tailed prairie dogs of the plains. Colonies studied in eastern Colorado by Tileston and Lechleitner were subdivided into smaller assemblages by topographic features. These groups appeared to be similar to the city "wards" described by King. These wards were again subdivided into smaller groups similar to the coteries of King.

The white-tailed prairie dog, commonly seen in mountain parks and valleys above 7,000 feet of elevation is generally found in small, isolated colonies. The Gunnison's prairie dog also lives in isolated pairs or widely separated families. Neither subspecies appears to have the close companionship that is common to the black-tailed prairie dogs.

The white-tailed prairie dogs watched by Tileston in Jackson County, Colorado, however, lived in loosely organized family groups which he called *clans*. Territorial boundaries between them were not evident, although specific burrow systems tended to be occupied by a particular clan. When members of another clan approached these burrows, there were no displays of antagonism by the owners.

More study, however, is necessary before the social behavior of prairie dogs is thoroughly understood. Little information is available on the white-tailed species, which once densely populated the mountains of Colorado, Arizona, and New Mexico. Behavior and social organization of the restricted colonies that now remain may not be the same as it was in the original towns, which covered thousands of acres.

Modern prairie dog towns seldom exceed one hundred or more acres and those that remain are generally in rough or rolling country where plant life varies with slope, exposure, and moisture supply. These physical variations in the landscape are conducive to the formation of wards. When prairie dog towns originally extended for miles over the level, uniformly vegetated short-grass prairies, wards probably were indistinct, if they existed at all.

Ronald E. Smith, for example, found aggressiveness and territorial disputes among black-tailed prairie dogs in Kansas so infrequent he was unable to draw any conclusions. Tileston and Lechleitner also found few territorial disputes in a colony of black-tailed prairie dogs near Fort Collins, Colorado. They suggested that there were fewer disputes in the Colorado colony they studied, which had been established for many years, than in King's study site, where the boundaries were just being established.

Although the social territory appears to endure in some towns as a heritage handed down through generations, we know relatively little about what happens when a town disappears and then is reinhabited a few years later. One study of this kind was made by Duncan P. Himes, who introduced black-tailed prairie dogs into an area where prairie dogs had formerly lived. After the original inhabitants died in 1963, burrowing owls and rabbits had selected the better burrows and kept them open.

Burrowing owl family. These long-legged birds live in abandoned prairie dog burrows and are amusing to watch. (Alfred M. Bailey, Denver Museum of Natural History)

When new prairie dogs were introduced in 1965, they used the burrows that had been occupied and disputes arose between the owls and prairie dogs. Coteries were established by the new prairie dogs, but the study did not make clear if these coteries covered essentially the same areas as the original ones.

In any prairie dog town there are, of course, many daily happenings. In a town I noted for several years near Briggsdale, Colorado, the prairie dogs were above ground by 5:30 or 6:00 A.M. on clear days in June and July. Usually they spent the first half hour sitting on or near their mounds, reconnoitering. If their survey of the landscape revealed a coyote, they gave the alarm call and all of them remained close to their burrows. At the approach of the coyote they disappeared into the ground and sometimes did not emerge before a half hour had passed.

Normally the prairie dogs engaged in kissing, grooming, and watching for thirty minutes or more. Then they waddled out to the grass sward to eat blue grama, buffalo grass, tumble grass, and pigweed. When eating blue grama leaves and buffalo grass stolons (a runner over the ground) they kept their noses to the earth for minutes at a time. When they clipped a stalk of a taller plant, such as June grass or western wheat grass, they sat upright with the stem in one or both paws, nibbled momentarily, and then cast the stem aside.

61

The feeding period, including interruptions by alarm calls and other activities, generally lasted until ten o'clock in the morning on warm days. When it was cool and cloudy, the prairie dogs fed intermittently throughout the day. They usually ate intensely during the two hours preceding sundown.

As the young prairie dogs became self-sufficient, there was much running, playing, and exploring around the home mounds. As they grew older, playing diminished and occasional chases ended in brief fights. The adults were often antagonistic to the young and were inclined to spend more time feeding, wandering around, basking in the sun, and cleaning out their burrows. On days when thunder showers moistened the ground, the adults repaired their mounds with fresh soil and tamped the entrances of their craters hard with their noses.

Several families of burrowing owls lived in the prairie dog town. It was always amusing to see the adult and three or four young owls standing side by side on their long legs at the top of the mound. The prairie dog youngsters did the same on their mounds, often in groups of three to six. Both owls and prairie dogs seemed to be curious about everything that moved in the town.

Eagles occasionally came down from the chalk bluffs that paralleled

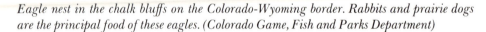

Eagle nest in the chalk bluffs on the Colorado-Wyoming border. Rabbits and prairie dogs are the principal food of these eagles. (Colorado Game, Fish and Parks Department)

the Wyoming-Colorado border a few miles north of the town. When these large predators coursed over the area, the place immediately became a ghost town. Just before sundown, marsh hawks making their last forays of the day caused similar alarms. Jackrabbits abroad at that time, however, elicited only mild curiosity from the prairie dogs.

The growth of the young prairie dogs in this town was amazing. By late September some were nearly adult size, although they did not appear to be as fat as their elders. Weight studies of prairie dogs indicate that the young seldom have the same weight as adults by fall. In their second summer, however, yearling prairie dogs equal the older animals in weight.

White-tailed prairie dogs studied in Wyoming by Eugene B. Bakko and Larry N. Brown gained weight rapidly and approached adult size by late October, when they ceased surface activity. Their parents had stopped one or two months earlier. Tileston and Lechleitner found the weights of white-tailed prairie dogs highly variable, depending on the season and on the amount of food in their stomachs at weighing time. The weights of males ranged from 750 grams to 1,700 grams (26.4 to 59.9 ounces); females ranged from 675 to 1,200 grams (28.8 to 42.3 ounces). The young weighed between 100 and 150 grams (3.5 to 5.3 ounces) when they first emerged from their burrows in early June. Before they became dormant in the fall, their weights were nearly equal to those of adults in early spring. At no time, however, did the weights of youngsters and adults overlap.

The average weight of twenty male Zuni prairie dogs collected by Theodore H. Scheffer at Flagstaff, Arizona, April 19 to June 4 was 20.6 ounces. The average weight of twenty-five females was 19.6 ounces. The weight of the young was not reported.

The breaking of family ties starts with the weaning of the litter. The mother soon leaves home and occupies another burrow. She may move out of the family territory and establish a home at the edge of the town. Meanwhile, the youngsters grow and begin to go their separate ways.

Before summer is ended many of them establish holdings in burrows that have been abandoned by former owners. Others, particularly the yearlings, may migrate long distances and establish colonies in territories where food supplies are abundant.

Prairie dogs are predominantly vegetarians. They eat a great variety of plants and are especially fond of wheat grasses and plants of the goosefoot family. All parts of the plant are eaten: leaves, stems, flowers, seeds, and roots. The summer diet of the prairie dog also includes grasshoppers and other succulent insects. The young seem to enjoy chasing insects that hop or run rapidly.

Prairie dogs exert a certain amount of control over insect populations by affecting the plants on which insects live and by eating the insects themselves. C. Y. McCulloch found that nearly three fourths of the prairie dogs collected near Billings, Montana, in May had larvae of noctuid moths in their stomachs.

When food is scarce, prairie dogs eat almost any plant that is available. The list of plants reported in scientific studies of their food habits is almost endless. The grasses they prefer are western wheat grass, blue grama, buffalo grass, six-weeks fescue, sand dropseed, foxtail, and various brome grasses and the seeds of grasses. If cockleburs are available, prairie dogs will open the spiny burs to get the seeds. When they are not able to find green herbaceous plants, they eat prickly-pear cactus, four-wing saltbush, rabbit brush, and the bark of oak sprouts.

Prairie dogs consume considerable quantities of roots. I am inclined to believe that they obtain substantial amounts of food when they dig their burrows. Roots sometimes are mixed with the soil in their crater mounds to form a kind of adobe which is hard and durable. But various tunnels I have excavated were dug through dense root systems of grasses. These roots were not visible in the vicinity of the mounds. Did the prairie dogs eat them as they dug their burrows?

Digging, of course, is more than an avocation for prairie dogs. They are one of the most accomplished burrowing animals, and their engi-

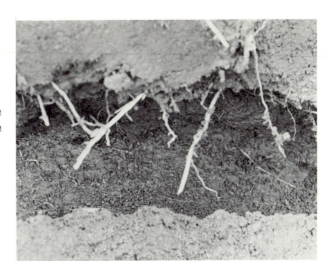

Part of a new burrow from which grass roots have not yet been clipped.

neering practices have excited the curiosity of men from the time of the early explorers to the present.

Various authors have received credit for writing the classical description of the prairie dog burrow system. The burrow excavated by W. H. Osgood and described by C. Hart Merriam in the *Yearbook of Agriculture* for 1901 descended at a sharp angle for 14 feet 7 inches and had an overall length of 24 feet. The average diameter was 4½ inches, and the prairie dog had dug a listening post or vestibule about three feet below the ground. At a depth of fourteen feet, along the horizontal part of the burrow, Osgood discovered a grass-lined nest chamber 9 by 11 inches.

On the basis of what other workers have observed, there does not appear to be a "typical" prairie dog burrow system. Indeed, as N. Hollister stated in his *Systematic Account of the Prairie Dogs,* "the burrows vary greatly according to local necessities." B. C. Jillson, for example, traced the burrow of a captive prairie dog under a coal shed and found that it was less than eighteen inches deep.

No one can deny that a completed prairie dog burrow is extensive. Zebulon Pike, the discoverer of Pike's Peak, learned this many years ago. He reported that he had 140 kettles of water poured into a prairie dog hole with no results. (He did not mention the capacity of the kettles.)

65

Young prairie dog with dirt on its fur after digging.

In spite of the great labor involved in excavating a prairie dog tunnel system, numerous workers have done it. B. E. Foster dug out a Gunnison's prairie dog burrow near Prescott, Arizona, in order to study the prairie dog's means of escaping drowning. In another flooding study, L. C. Whitehead excavated a prairie dog colony near Barstow, Texas. In a salt-grass pasture he found burrows with a general depth of 24 to 32 inches where the normal level of the water table was about 50 inches below the ground.

66

One of the most extensive digging jobs was recently done by Maxwell Wilcomb, Jr., in order to study the arthropod inhabitants of prairie dog burrows in Oklahoma. He dug thirteen burrows and found tunnels varying in length from 15½ feet to 86 feet and ranging in depth from 34 inches to 73 inches. Most tunnels had a single entrance through either a domelike mound or a mound with a crater. One listening room, or diverticulum, as Wilcomb called it, was twenty inches inside the entrance; another was eight feet from the entrance. The listening room is a chamber where the prairie dog can stop, listen, and turn around.

A pet prairie dog. Its claws are built for digging.

Other burrows had no pocket or "turn around" room. Some of the tunnels turned to the right about three feet below the entrance; others did not turn. Three tunnels had nest chambers that varied from 1 to 1½ feet in length and from 8 to 12 inches in width.

Wilcomb found one tunnel with a median ridge on the floor. He believed that the refinement of leveling the floor and enlarging the bore would have been done later. He found one place where two burrow systems, apparently originating separately, had come together and were being used as a single system. He concluded, however, that tunnel systems were not usually connected in a colony. He detected that the occupant, by plugging and unplugging various branches and intersections, could easily suit the design of his home to his immediate needs.

The subterranean connections discovered by King were found to vary from season to season. He saw some of his marked prairie dogs enter one mound and appear at another. He interpreted this as evidence of underground connections between burrows. He also blocked the openings of burrows and saw prairie dogs appear at other entrances with soil on their claws, indicating they had dug out a plugged portion of the burrow system. Since a single burrow may have several openings, the appearance of the same prairie dog at different mounds may not be proof of connections between burrow systems.

The number of burrows per colony varies greatly, depending on the prairie dog population, type of soil, and availability of forage. In his study of two wards in the Black Hills, King found 57 burrows per acre in 1948 and 52.5 per acre in 1950. Tileston and Lechleitner found an average of 41.9 burrow entrances per acre in a black-tailed prairie dog study site in eastern Colorado. An average of only 5.2 burrow entrances, however, were used during the peak of animal numbers. These same workers found 21.9 entrances per acre in a white-tailed prairie dog colony but only 5 entrances were used, indicating 1 entrance per active animal.

I have been unable to find any published report of the number of

A dome mound without a crater rim. This black-tailed prairie dog simply throws soil in all directions.

Burrow entrance molded by prairie dogs pressing their noses into the moist soil.

nests per colony, ward, or coterie. My study of the literature suggests that about one burrow in three may be expected to contain a prairie dog nest.

Excavated nest chambers show great variation in the amounts of dried grass used for bedding material. Some have a thin layer of shredded grass on the floor of the chamber which may be 18 inches long, 12 inches wide, and 14 or 15 inches high. Other nest chambers are almost completely filled with dried grass. Nests of the Zuni prairie dog excavated by Theodore H. Scheffer (1947) near Flagstaff, Arizona, were composed entirely of pine needles, even though grass was available in the vicinity.

69

The spare earth entrance or escape hole is not marked with a mound of earth. Prairie dogs are well acquainted with the locations of these hidden entrances.

This burrow, made by white-tailed prairie dogs in Utah, has seven entrances. Shrubs around the mound are Nuttall's saltbush.

The mounds of excavated soil around burrow entrances of black-tailed prairie dogs are either dome-shaped or crater-shaped. Dome mounds are round piles of subsoil with the burrow entrance in the top. They vary from 1 to 3 feet in height and may be from 2 to 10 feet in diameter at the base. Crater mounds are conical and frequently composed of a mixture of subsoil, topsoil, and debris which consists of roots brought up from below or grass scraped up from near the edge of the mound.

70

Black-tailed prairie dogs spend much time shaping their mounds. They kick soil and debris out of the tunnel or push it along the ground with their folded forelegs. When the soil is workable after rain storms, they tamp the soil. Smith gave this description of the process: "The prairie dog carries or pushes the soil and debris to the proper place and then on all fours, with body, neck, and head rigid but with the shoulders hunched, forcefully rams its nose into the moist material. Sometimes the head is held slightly down so the bridge of the nose and the forehead do most of the packing." The nose prints are sometimes so evenly spaced they make interesting designs around the tunnel entrance.

The mounds of the white-tailed prairie dog are usually not shaped but are merely large piles of dirt surrounding the entrance hole. They consist of subsoil, since these prairie dogs do not bring in surface soil and vegetable debris from the outside.

The Zuni prairie dogs simply pile the excavated soil into a ramp that resembles the tailings miners leave on the slopes in the Rocky Mountains. They do not work the mound into a crater or tamp the entrance with their noses. Similarly, Gunnison's prairie dogs kick the dirt out of their burrows and make no attempt at packing. Since they collect no soil from outside, the length of their burrows may be estimated by the size of the mounds.

In many prairie dog towns, I have noted that about one third or even one half of the burrows have no mounds. Some of these moundless burrows are plugged with soil. Others are left open as escape hatches in case water flows into the burrow from the main entrance. They also serve as escape tunnels if enemies surprise the prairie dogs when they are away from the main entrances.

Prairie dogs are relatively large rodents and consequently have fewer enemies than mice, chipmunks, or kangaroo rats. Their principal predators are black-footed ferrets, badgers, coyotes, eagles, and rough-legged hawks.

Formerly, the prairie dog's most dangerous natural enemy was the

The black-footed ferret hunts mostly at night in prairie dog towns. It is one of the rarest animals in North America and is in danger of extinction. (National Park Service)

Badgers in mountainous country are enemies of the white-tailed prairie dogs.

black-footed ferret. These animals are large, weasel-like, and about the size of a mink. They are now among the rarest mammals in North America and can be identified by the yellowish buff upper parts, the black mask on the face and the black feet and black-tipped tail.

The black-footed ferret originally lived in the Great Plains and adjoining territories, and its range nearly coincided with that of the prairie dog. Once in my life I had the memorable experience of seeing a black-footed ferret in the wild—at Bates Hole in Wyoming. It sat upright and stared at me with green, glittering eyes and then slithered through the grass with a sinuous serpentine movement toward a rodent burrow.

Harold C. Smith reported he once saw a black-footed ferret enter a burrow on the ranch where he lived in Montana. The whole town erupted with chattering prairie dogs, some of which dug out plugs of earth from escape tunnels. Pandemonium reigned, and the inhabitants appeared to be terror-stricken.

Ferrets are nocturnal animals that kill at night. They dig into a plugged prairie dog burrow and then drag the prey to an abandoned burrow that they use as a den.

Although ferrets have the reputation of being killers, they have always been relatively rare in number and have never been able to reduce seriously the prairie dog population. Persecution of prairie dogs by ranchers, farmers, and federal predator control men has almost exterminated the black-footed ferrets, and only a few remain. However, in South Dakota where prairie dogs are still abundant, they can be found.

Badgers are also enemies of the prairie dogs. Their digging results in terrible destruction of prairie dog towns. They are able to excavate several shallow burrows in a night and seem to determine by smell if the burrow is occupied. During the day badgers have been seen pursuing prairie dogs to their dens. Most of the badger's excavation, however, is done after dark and may also be for rabbits, ground squirrels, and mice.

Formerly badgers were common throughout the Great Plains and were most numerous in areas where prairie dogs lived. Badger diggings may be found all through the year in the plains states. Even in the mountains, prairie dogs are not immune to their plundering. Longhurst, after studying prairie dogs in Colorado, stated that a female badger with her two half-grown youngsters dug out fourteen burrows of the Gunnison's prairie dog in six days. The burrows were in a meadow at an elevation of 9,500 feet.

Koford believed that the principal effect of badgers on prairie dogs is their hindrance of the expansion of their towns. When prairie dogs begin construction of their burrows, the holes are shallow and easy to excavate.

There have been numerous accounts of badger-coyote partnerships in prairie dog towns throughout the years. Cahalane, for example, cited four observations of badgers and coyotes working together in the Theodore Roosevelt National Memorial Park in North Dakota and in the Badlands National Monument in South Dakota. Park rangers watched the two animals walk side by side or otherwise remain in close association. In one observation by rangers, both animals caught prairie dogs by rushing simultaneously into the colony. In another, the badger entered a hole and a prairie dog popped out a different entrance. The attending coyote apparently was not watchful and the prairie dog escaped. The question, "Are such associations between predatory animals of mutual benefit?" has not been satisfactorily resolved.

Alone, the coyote is a serious predator and, with bobcats, once probably exerted a significant curbing of prairie dog populations. Although coyotes have been persecuted in recent times, I have seen them or found their tracks in almost every prairie dog town I visited in the West. Coyotes also prey on rabbits, mice, ground squirrels, birds, and insects in prairie dog towns. (In eastern Colorado they even include watermelons in their diet.) The attraction of coyotes to dog towns at night, when the prairie dogs are below ground, is probably accounted for by the abundance of rabbits and nocturnal rodents.

John Patterson, in charge of the north unit of the Theodore Roosevelt National Memorial Park, told me about an amusing observation he made of a young coyote stalking a chirping prairie dog. The coyote made a most careful approach, stealthily crawling on his belly while the prairie dog chirped louder and louder. Finally, the coyote could wait no longer and dashed madly to the mound. The prairie dog, with flickering tail, dived instantly into its burrow.

Golden eagles have always been successful predators of prairie dogs. When I did range research in northeastern Colorado, the eagles came down from the Chalk Bluffs along the Wyoming border to sit on fence posts near the prairie dog towns. Although I never saw an eagle catch a prairie dog, eagle nests in the Bluffs always contained remnants of jackrabbit, cottontail, and prairie dog bodies while their fledglings were growing up.

In a study of food remains in and around eagle nests in northern Colorado, D. O. D'Ostilio discovered that rabbits were the most common prey of eagles when prairie dogs were scarce. At one nest, however, he found that prairie dogs apparently provided the most abundant food.

Koford pointed out that the tendency of eagles to nest in separate territories several miles apart limits certain hunting areas to single pairs of eagles. They are such capable hunters, however, that one pair could eliminate all the prairie dogs from a town. He also pointed out that the taking of adult female prairie dogs early in spring when they are pregnant or have dependent young would have a greater effect on their populations than taking females in summer.

Hawks, including ferruginous, red-tailed, and marsh hawks, are not as predatory on prairie dogs as are the eagles, but all these hawks, and prairie falcons too, are capable of taking juvenile prairie dogs. I have seen marsh hawks kill mature jackrabbits near Nunn, Colorado, which were certainly much larger than juvenile prairie dogs, and have flushed them from eating cottontails while the rabbits were still alive.

Among the squatters or uninvited inhabitants of dog town are large

75

Rattlesnakes and their associations with burrowing owls and prairie dogs are legendary. The snakes hibernate in abandoned burrows.

Bull snakes eat young prairie dogs and rabbits, mice, and other rodents in prairie dog towns. This bull snake, on the Wichita Mountains Wildlife Refuge, was more than six feet long.

snakes which feed on prairie dogs. Rattlesnakes have been reported from the time of Lewis and Clark to the present. Numerous records of rattlesnakes in prairie dog towns are included in the monumental rattlesnake study by Laurence M. Klauber. Many of the other accounts I have read are so fantastic that I can only believe they are fictitious or based on conclusions reached by incompetent observers.

Ernest Thompson Seton wrote that prairie dogs will entomb a rattlesnake if they find it in a burrow. With regard to this, the following quotation from William M. Longhurst is of interest:

In an effort to get at the truth of this relationship, four rattlesnakes *(Crotalus viridens)* were kept, tethered by cords tied to their tails, in the burrows of prairie dogs for an average period of four days each. In no case was there any indication of the dogs attempting to bury the snakes.

Throughout the day the snakes generally remained in their burrows, but at night they came out and usually crawled away to the length of the cord. As nearly as could be determined the prairie dogs remained in the burrow as long as the snake blocked the exit, but when the snake left they deserted the burrow and did not return for several days after the snake was removed. Even in burrows with two entrances they did not attempt to bury the snake. On two occasions rattlers were discovered seeking refuge during the day in prairie dog burrows, but in each instance they were abandoned burrows.

Similarly, King on two occasions:

. . . tied a string around a rattlesnake's head and staked it out in the town. Although the snake's primary effort was to escape, prairie dogs came up and fed within a foot of it, often within the length of the string. They were curious about the snake and approached it cautiously, sometimes calling as they ran off and then returned to the snake. Prairie dogs never barked at snakes. When one rattlesnake was released, a pup followed it and even pawed at its tail as it crawled away. Such behavior can hardly be characteristic of a prey species towards its predator.

King also staked out a bull snake in the Shirttail Canyon town in the

77

Black Hills. It caused no more alarm among the prairie dogs than did the rattlesnake. He wrote, however, that, soon after the snakes emerge from hibernation, both rattlesnakes and bull snakes probably prey on young prairie dogs.

Years ago, Robert Blight referred to an article by Charles U. Becker in *Field and Stream* which told how the author saw a rattlesnake disappearing into a burrow. An excited prairie dog bobbed up and raced around the entrance, barking incessantly. Within minutes twenty prairie dogs assembled around the burrow, barked for a while, and then, as if started by a signal, scratched dirt into the hole, filled it quickly, and pressed the soil level with the surface with their noses. Whatever may be the merit of this account, it makes a good story.

In their report of a plant study on the Wichita Mountains Wildlife Refuge in Oklahoma, Osborn and Allen concluded that increase in stature and density of grass cover, following removal of cattle, forced a prairie dog colony to occupy a denuded central area surrounded by unpalatable three-awn grass. Unsuitable food in the barren area brought about a decline in prairie dog numbers, and rattlesnakes probably killed the rest. Refuge Manager Ernest J. Greenwalt noted that the last few prairie dogs were reluctant to enter their burrows, and on investigation he located seven rattlers by their buzzing. Three snakes were twisted out of the holes with sticks.

I am inclined to believe that bull snakes may also have been a factor in eliminating prairie dogs from other towns in the Wichita Refuge. On my last visit there I encountered some of the largest bull snakes I have ever seen. One that I photographed and followed for an hour measured approximately 6½ feet. A snake of this size can destroy an entire clutch of young rabbits at a time and certainly would have no difficulty in swallowing young prairie dogs still in their nests.

The old legend of rattlesnakes, prairie dogs, and burrowing owls living in the same burrow still persists. The owls, of course, are professional squatters in prairie dog land, principally because the prairie dogs provide habitable holes for them, but early accounts of the three animals living together have now been discounted by recent and more accurate observations.

The notion that owls go down a hole and cause a rattlesnake to buzz has been refuted by ornithologist Lewis Wayne Walker ("Rattlesnakes and Owls") in an ingenious study. He dug away the earth from an owl nest and covered it with a glass plate so that hatching and growth of the young could be observed. When the nestling owls were disturbed, they made a buzz resembling that of a rattlesnake.

In animal communities of such long duration as the prairie dog town, it is inevitable that other animals will use the area in spite of anything the prairie dogs can do. On the original prairie the bison found the towns

Bison once lived in countless millions on the plains, grazing in prairie dog towns and using the mounds as wallows to deter insect pests.

acceptable as grazing places because of the abundance of forbs that sprang up as the prairie dogs reduced the supply of competing grasses. These forbs were generally palatable, rich in nitrogen, and furnished variety in the bison diet.

The bison also found convenient wallowing places in prairie dog towns. When their winter wool had been shed and insects became pestiferous, the huge beasts pawed the prairie dog mounds and rolled in the dust or mud to acquire a protective coating.

One can easily imagine the devastation of mounds when bison herds of almost incomprehensible numbers stampeded through prairie dog towns. The pounding feet of thousands of beasts would have made the earth tremble and left the soil bare of any living thing. Even a herd of less than 300 bison, which I have observed on numerous occasions in the Black Hills of South Dakota, can denude the earth so that some areas resemble plowed fields. There is nothing the prairie dogs can do about the bison wallowing, pawing, and feeding. The dogs retire to their burrows or go about their business of grazing, if the bison are ruminating or moving slowly.

Denudation by the bison worked sometimes to the advantage of the prairie dogs. The soil disturbance prepared the ground for future growth of forbs (characteristic of early plant succession stages) that produced palatable food for prairie dogs. This modification of the vegetation also created temporary habitats favorable for grazing by ground squirrels, rabbits, mice, and pronghorns.

Next to the bison, the pronghorns, which once numbered in the millions, were the most important grazers on the plains. They too found prairie dog towns congenial places for feeding because of the greater abundance of forbs. In the Dakotas, where tall-grass prairie still remains, I have noted that pronghorns seem to be attracted to heavily grazed dog towns which support weedy types of plants.

The communal life in prairie dog towns offers exciting opportunities for the study of food chains and the web of life in nature. The co-dwellers

Pronghorns resting in a Montana prairie dog town. The pronghorns eat the herbs that appear when prairie dogs have removed the grasses.

in dog towns are exceedingly numerous and varied. Some, like the rattle-snake, burrowing owl, and box turtle, are there because of food, shelter, protection from predators, and the need for places of hibernation. Others, like the prairie chicken and sharp-tailed grouse, are there to en-joy dancing grounds that the bare spaces in dog town provide during their courting season in late winter. Some, like the jays and magpies in Zuni prairie dog towns, may be there just out of curiosity. But if we knew the self-interests of all the creatures, furred or feathered, that associate with prairie dogs, we would have a better understanding of nature and her workings.

Burrowing owls are grotesque creatures, owing to their long legs and short tails. The families are ludicrous and endearing, especially when the young group together on a prairie dog mound, standing five to seven in a row with their parents. Frequently, one or more of the young owls will dash among the prairie dogs in pursuit of a grasshopper.

81

Oftentimes antagonism will develop between prairie dogs and burrowing owls. In a study made in eastern Colorado, Duncan P. Himes reported that prairie dogs sought the shelter of burrows when attacked by owls; on other occasions the owls flew away when attacked by prairie dogs. These "attacks" consisted of the prairie dog rushing at the owl or the owl swooping over the prairie dog with a raucous squeal.

I do not believe prairie dogs are really afraid of owls. They simply dive into their burrows at the swoop of an owl because they are conditioned to danger from flying hawks and eagles. When I chased burrowing owls all over the landscape near Kadoka, North Dakota, while attempting to photograph them in flight, the prairie dogs showed instant alarm as the birds skimmed rapidly over the ground above them, but, as soon as the owls perched, the prairie dogs began to graze within a few feet of mounds on which the owls perched.

Owl-inhabited burrows can be distinguished easily from burrows occupied by prairie dogs. The owl's front yard is nearly always littered with bones, pieces of fur, owl pellets, horse dung, and other trash. Its burrow is almost invariably supplied with dried horse and cow manure. When the owl does a cleanup job in its hole, a veritable shower of debris is scratched and thrown out of the entrance.

It is probable that young prairie dogs in their burrows occasionally furnish a meal for the owls. In turn, the prairie dogs may rob the owls of their eggs. And, almost certainly, large snakes eat the eggs of owls as well as the young of prairie dogs and owls.

On account of the abundant weedy areas in prairie dog towns, the environment is favorable for many seed-eating birds and for insects which attract insectivorous birds. Common bird visitors in dog towns are meadow larks, horned larks, lark buntings, mourning doves, Alaskan longspurs, McCown's longspurs, Sprague's pipits, and American magpies. The grass sward is generally thin, and insects are easily seen and captured. Magpies will examine freshly excavated soil for insects, lizards, and other small animals that may have been thrown out of the

Western meadow larks are found in almost every prairie dog town on the plains.

Magpies search for grasshoppers in prairie dog towns and look for insects in the debris dug out of tunnels.

ground by prairie dog digging. Killdeers nest sometimes in prairie dog towns located near ponds. The prairie dogs pay little attention to these birds, even the large magpies, which chase grasshoppers when they are common in late summer. The extent to which the prairie dogs affect the food supply, cover, and nesting habitat of the birds, however, is not well known. Nor is it known how extensively the birds affect the prairie dog environment.

Jackrabbits and cottontails are numerous in and around prairie dog towns. The jackrabbits like the visibility that results from the grass-clipping activities of the prairie dogs. In early evening jackrabbits run in tandem along established paths. At this time prairie dogs are taking

Cottontails on the plains and in the mountains find prairie dog burrows useful for refuge from enemies, for shelter, and for nesting places for their young.

their last look of the day, and the activities of jackrabbits seem to disturb the dogs and make them stay close to their mounds.

Smith recently described an interesting activity of jackrabbits in a Kansas prairie dog town. He wrote:

In early morning six to ten jackrabbits would congregate at various seemingly established places near the edge of dogtown and engage in a sort of play activity; while four to eight rabbits sat in a circle, two others would run around this circle, one following the other by about ten feet, and these two would "take their places" in the circle and two others would take off. All the while gutteral sounds would be audible from the group of rabbits. During such activity, prairie dogs would sit on their mounds and watch. This happened two to three times a week in summer and the prairie dogs seemingly always remained curious about it, just as I did.

Cottontails use abandoned burrows for shelter, for escape from enemies, and for raising their young. I learned this when I used pellet counts in making a rabbit census east of Fort Collins, Colorado, over a period of several years. I threw a one-foot-square wire frame at random in fifty places in each area being sampled. When the rabbit pellet count averaged three per square foot it indicated a population of approximately one rabbit per acre.

In one prairie dog town sampled, the pellet count signified a cottontail population of nearly two per acre. Then the prairie dogs in the area were poisoned by a rodent control crew. Their burrows were filled with soil and obliterated by cattle trampling. At the end of five years the pellet count taken indicated less than one rabbit for every ten acres.

In the location of the former prairie dog town my two sons and I made rabbit shelters by laying old boiler pipe, 4 inches in diameter and 8 to 12 feet long. We also improvised shelters with poles, old fence posts, pieces of sheet metal, and old barn doors supported on two-by-four lumber. Within three years the rabbit population was back to approximately one rabbit for every two acres. We were convinced that cottontails benefit from shelter, whether supplied by human efforts or those of the prairie dogs.

Many other animals also take advantage of the burrows in dog towns. Various lizards and the tiger salamander use them for escape from enemies and to protect themselves from the drying winds of the prairie. Toads are commonly found in burrows, and ornate box turtles use them for refuges and for hibernating places in winter.

Insects of various orders are abundant in prairie dog towns. Grasshoppers are usually seen in late summer. Smith recorded robber flies, bluebottle flies, and darkling beetles in and around burrow openings. In a recent visit to a prairie dog town west of Fort Collins, Colorado, I counted nearly fifty of these beetles (Eleodes) in the entrance of a burrow. Smith believed that the beetles are eaten by the prairie dogs in May and early June.

In an extensive study of the arthropod inhabitants in a prairie dog town, Wilcomb excavated thirteen burrows in Oklahoma. From these he collected 33,137 arthropods representing twelve families and including twenty-nine species of beetles or their larvae. He also collected representatives of eighteen families of arachnida, including pseudoscorpions, spiders, mites, and ticks.

Bombardier beetles, black widow spiders, eyeless beetles, camel-back crickets, and prairie dog fleas were indicative of the variety of animal

White penstamon, a common forb that prairie dogs eat.

life in the prairie dog burrows. Wilcomb reported that many of these creatures walked into the tunnels. Some were carried in with dung and vegetable debris—possibly as eggs that had been deposited on these materials outside the burrows—and others arrived there in the fur of the prairie dogs.

Obviously the burrow climate was favorable for many of these arthropod inhabitants. When the surface soil temperature varied from 75.5 to 119.5 degrees Fahrenheit, the average temperature 41 to 49 inches below ground was 80 degrees Fahrenheit. Relative humidity of the burrow air July 31 through August 4 was 88.3 per cent. In late January and early February, soil temperature at depths of 42 to 66 inches varied only between 49 and 51.5 degrees Fahrenheit. Burrow humidity averaged 88 per cent. Thus, prairie dogs create an environment not only favorable to themselves but also beneficial to other creatures.

The harvester ant, *Pogonomyrmex occidentalis,* that builds mounds rivaling those of the prairie dog, provides an interesting example of the mutual advantages of association between different types of animals in prairie dog towns. I once counted the ant mounds in various stages of vegetation recovery on the Great Plains, which I reported in *Ecology* in

1944. I found the largest number of mounds to be in the intermediate stages of plant succession, which are generally maintained by livestock overgrazing or by prairie dog habitation. In these intermediate stages the ants compete with birds, rodents, and other insects for seeds. They compete with the prairie dogs for grasses, since the ants cut down the grasses that germinate and start to grow in their cleared circles. On the other hand, when an ant colony dies, it leaves a substratum conducive to rapid invasion of buffalo grass and annual forbs with leaves and seeds that are relished by prairie dogs, antelopes, insects, and birds.

An abundance of seeds and large insects make prairie dog towns an attractive place for ground squirrels and mice. Although the ground squirrels dig their own burrows for hibernation, they use prairie dog burrows for refuges from enemies and bad weather and eat many of the beetles and grasshoppers.

The grasshopper mouse, *Onychomys leucogaster,* also eats insects in prairie dog towns. Its activities interfere little with those of the prairie dogs, since they take place at night. The prairie deer mouse, *Peromyscus maniculatus,* lives in almost every prairie dog town in the West. Along with the kangaroo rat, these mice frequently dig into the granaries at the edge of harvester ant mounds and rob the ants of their stored seeds.

Seed production and growth of vegetation in dog town, of course, vary greatly with seasonal weather. These variations influence the lives and activities of the prairie dogs and their animal associates. Several summers of above-average rainfall can increase grass growth faster than the prairie dogs can control it. The plants may become so dense that the land is no longer suitable as a habitat, and the prairie dogs may migrate or be reduced in numbers by predators. Prolonged summer droughts, on the other hand, are not necessarily detrimental to prairie dogs, although scarcity of food may cause the towns to expand to new territory or even result in the migration of prairie dogs to areas with more abundant food supplies.

Prairie dogs are capable of living for long periods without water or even

Prickly-pear cactus serves as emergency food for prairie dogs when drought reduces the supply of grasses and forbs.

dew on the grass. Like kangaroo rats, they are capable of manufacturing some metabolic water from the food they eat. Green plants also supply some of the water necessary for their lives. When grasses and forbs are completely dried, they eat prickly-pear cactus and the bark of shrubs.

During the severe drought of 1939 in northeastern Colorado, when the grass was dry enough to burn at night, grasshoppers were very abundant. The grasshoppers subsisted on dried leaves and the twigs of rabbit brush and four-wing saltbush. I noted that prairie dogs caught more grasshoppers than usual, possibly as a moisture supplement to the grass roots they dug out of the ground.

Prairie dogs also vary their activities according to daily changes in the weather. On days when the temperature exceeds 100 degrees Fahrenheit they are active but make frequent trips to their burrows. King noted that prairie dogs in the Black Hills spent 15 per cent of their active day inside burrows and 42 per cent underground when the temperature exceeded 100, at which time the soil surface was 113 and the burrow temperature one foot below was 74 degrees.

88

Summer

During slow drizzles on summer days prairie dogs remain active, eating and repairing their mounds. During heavy rainstorms, however, they stay underground. When the rain stops, they begin scratching surface soil onto their mounds and tamping the entrances hard with their noses.

Prairie dogs like sunshine and warm summer weather. This is when they exhibit their gregarious instincts. Their town becomes a vital moving ecosystem in which mammals, birds, insects, reptiles, and plants determine their destinies, as they once did when the bison roamed the land.

Black-tailed prairie dogs basking in sunshine in North Dakota.

Prairie dogs grow fat in autumn in preparation for periods of winter quiescence or dormancy.

Autumn

IN PRAIRIE DOG WORLD early autumn is the colorful season of abundancy. On the plains and in the mountains dry weather generally prevails, and hardy asters, goldenrods, evening stars, henbanes, and different varieties of rabbit brush put on a spectacular show.

The yucca stalks bear large seed pods—the cattle have not eaten them. The pads of prickly-pear cactus, swollen with summer moisture, are nibbled by the prairie dogs even before the blue grama has lost its purple tinge and the morning frosts have turned the prickly heads of coneflower to gray.

Some years the grasshoppers appear in hordes and provide great sport for the prairie dogs, which "field" the low-flying insects or chase them among the grasses. Food of any kind is important, for the fattening period must soon end and the partial fast of winter will require the use of energy stored from forbs and grasses eaten during the summer and autumn harvest.

In the mountains many adult white-tailed prairie dogs have already gone underground by September. Their young, however, still spend much time feeding and traveling on warm days. Some remain active until early November but retire soon after to the darkness of their burrows to spend winter beneath the snow.

Autumn activities among the black-tailed prairie dogs differ from those of summer. Although many hours are devoted to feeding, grooming is hardly done at all. Dominant males still patrol their territorial bound-

91

aries. In the morning, they are the first to appear above ground and at night the last to retire.

Juvenile prairie dogs are now nearly as large as adults and have outgrown many of the playful habits they exhibited as youngsters. They are able to sound danger signals with all the other members of the colony. If the town is crowded or food scarce, some of the adult males and the adventuresome juveniles migrate to new territories.

Extension of town limits is common when there is an increase in population. Crowding appears to be a partial cause of the expansion. Old

Town expansion. These prairie dogs have started new burrows and have not cut down the surrounding grass.

burrows at the edge of town are sometimes reconditioned because the land nearby has lain fallow and resulted in recovery of grass and palatable forbs.

Prairie dogs may make temporary summer use of burrows. These hillside burrows occupied in July are abandoned in favor of lower, greener pastures in September and October, with prairie dogs remaining in these autumn and winter homes until the grass is green again in spring.

Start of a new burrow. One of the first jobs is to clip the grass in the immediate vicinity to provide better visibility.

Actually, the boundaries of a prairie dog town are always changing from one year to the next. Towns go through periods of boom and bust based on yearly weather changes, shifts in the availability of edible plants, pressure by predators, and outbreaks of diseases. Some prairie dog colonies disappear for no apparent reason and become ghost towns.

I observed one town above the badlands of the Little Missouri River in 1968, which had expanded when prairie dogs began extensive grazing of the tall wheat grass and little bluestem around its border. Along some sections of the perimeter, as much as a hundred yards of grass had been removed by the prairie dogs during the summer. Adults were doing most of the clipping and still actively grazing in late September.

In the Theodore Roosevelt National Memorial Park, records have been kept of the acreage of prairie dog towns for several years. No town has been vacated since 1951, but several were reduced to only a handful of animals for a year or two. Then they recovered their former numbers.

Prairie dogs do start new towns, sometimes several miles from their old homes. Few people have ever seen these prairie dogs when they were traveling. Probably many individual wanderers get lost or are caught by predators. I knew one such prairie dog north of Nunn, Colorado. It lived all summer in a single burrow at least five miles from the nearest

Prairie dog town in the badlands of the Little Missouri River, North Dakota.

prairie dog town. I suspect that either an eagle or a coyote caught it in the autumn.

Mass migrations of prairie dogs are almost unknown. Possibly they were more common in the days of the bison when prairie dogs occurred by the millions on the Great Plains. Ernest Thompson Seton wrote that whole populations of dog towns sometimes abandoned home and its comforts and emigrated to new surroundings. Smith reported:

Professor Ronald L. McGregor of the Department of Botany at the University of Kansas tells me that he witnessed a mass migration of prairie dogs. They paid no attention to him or his horse and swept around him in such numbers that he was able to club many of them with a fence post. This occurred in Smith County, Kansas, and Webster County, Nebraska, near the culmination of a severe drought in the late afternoon in late July or early August of 1936.

Several years ago my friend Maynard Cummings, while working for the Fish and Wildlife Service, captured a Gunnison's prairie dog on top of Grand Mesa in western Colorado. This animal was found in a culvert under the Flowing Park Road at an elevation of approximately 10,000 feet. Maynard recently wrote to me, "If this dog got there on his own I think it is reasonable to assume he migrated up Kannah Creek. This would be a 20- to 30-mile hike from the nearest known prairie dog colonies down in the main valley of the Gunnison River near Whitewater. In addition to mileage it is an elevation rise of over 5,000 feet."

Migration does not necessarily explain the depopulation of prairie dog towns where numbers of animals gradually, or sometimes suddenly, disappear. As Koford pointed out, once the dogs are gone, it is easy to postulate such causes as predation by ferrets, disease, drought, hard winters, badgers, and lack of food. Prairie dog towns are sometimes secretly poisoned—I have known of three. Ranchers also have been known to carry plague-infested prairie dogs to plague-free areas on their own lands in order to transmit the disease.

Sylvatic plague, which infects prairie dogs, chipmunks, ground squirrels, and other rodents, can eradicate the animals over large areas. There is no evidence, however, that either this disease or the presence of parasites such as fleas, mites, and ticks will cause the prairie dogs to migrate. These parasites produce some discomfort in the animals, which occasionally take dust baths to free themselves of their tormentors.

We have seen that many uninvited guests use the prairie dog burrows at various times during the year. In autumn some of these animal intruders enter the burrows for hibernation. Ground beetles congregate sometimes in large numbers at tunnel entrances and presumably go below frost line in order to live out the winter. Ornate box turtles are frequently seen in burrows. Occasionally they seem to have difficulty emerging in spring if the tunnel they have entered is vertical instead of slanting.

Tiger salamanders and some toads use prairie dog burrows both as refuges and as places for hibernation. (The Great Plains toad and the spadefoot toad, however, do not regularly use prairie dog tunnels, since these animals are accomplished burrowers in their own right.) The salamanders are often found in dog towns near buffalo wallows or ponds that offer breeding places for the amphibians in early spring.

Tiger salamanders occasionally are found in prairie dog burrows. (National Park Service)

Thirteen-lined ground squirrels live in prairie dog towns but make their own burrows.

Autumn is also the time to find large numbers of ground-dwelling animals, such as snakes and mice, in prairie dog town. Bull snakes, hog-nose snakes, lined snakes, and rattlesnakes use abandoned burrows and find such food as thirteen-lined ground squirrels and various species of mice, whose numbers have increased during the reproductive season.

Although the ground squirrels dig their own hibernating burrows, they make instant use of prairie dog habitats when danger threatens. The prairie dogs usually ignore the ground squirrels but will sometimes growl and pursue them until they enter dog burrows. They probably never capture a ground squirrel.

Ronald E. Smith found in Kansas that hispid pocket mice, northern grasshopper mice, and deer mice used abandoned prairie dog burrows. In winter, he saw that burrows occupied by grasshopper mice could be identified by the grass that almost plugged the entrances, leaving only a hole about the size of a half dollar. Since grasshopper mice are nocturnal, their activities probably do not conflict with the prairie dogs.

Abandoned prairie dog burrows are used by black widow spiders. Note the prairie dog pellet suspended by spider web in the center of the entrance hole.

In eastern Colorado I have observed numerous black widow spiders in prairie dog towns. They spin their webs across the entrances of abandoned burrows. These webs are strong enough to support debris, including prairie dog pellets, kicked into the burrows by passing animals or blown in by the wind. I have also seen black widow spiders in prairie dog burrows in Oklahoma, Nebraska, and South Dakota.

Burrows used for web spinning by the spiders seem to be ignored by prairie dogs. I have seen webs with their debris that remained for two weeks without disturbance in the midst of a very active prairie dog town. The use of abandoned burrows is probably not due to any deliberate choice by the spiders. The construction of a web in a burrow used many times daily by the prairie dogs would naturally result in failure.

Burrows are sometimes abandoned when a prairie dog town is inundated by floods. Flooding is uncommon in the Great Plains in autumn. Once every twelve years or so a heavy rainstorm may continue for several days. I saw this happen one time in mid-October; the rain continued until temporary ponds were filled with several feet of water. More than half of a prairie dog town near Briggsdale, Colorado, was covered by water that remained throughout the winter. The prairie dogs were especially active in the dry sections of the town. I believe those from the flooded portion simply moved to the unflooded area.

In the fall of 1925, L. C. Whitehead studied a prairie dog town near Barstow, Texas, that was flooded by irrigation. The town was in a salt-grass pasture where the water table normally stood about four feet below the surface. While irrigation water temporarily covered two thirds of the town, the prairie dogs apparently perched in nest chambers only a foot below the surface. These air pockets saved their lives.

Fire is more likely than flood waters to strike prairie dog towns in autumn. Grasses are dry and humidity low, especially on the plains. Formerly, fires were set by Indians to stampede game animals. Conflagrations also started from unguarded campfires. Lightning has always been a cause of prairie fires. Modern prairie fires that spread over many square miles are caused by matches and cigarettes tossed from automobiles. None of these, however, appears to be catastrophic for prairie dogs.

Like the hills of the harvester ants, prairie dog mounds have no plants growing on them. And by late autumn, much of the town may be grazed by the animals so closely that little grass remains for burning. The prairie dogs, of course, merely retire to the safety of their burrows until the fire has passed.

If the plant cover is destroyed by fire, prairie dogs resort to digging roots of forbs and grasses. Root digging is rare when green plants are available, but if fire removes the prairie dogs' surface forage supply, their digging becomes conspicuous. The soil pits excavated by them usually are 1 to 3 inches deep, but sometimes they go to depths of 6 inches or more and resemble the beginnings of new burrows.

Most of the subterranean digging by prairie dogs is completed by early autumn, although I have seen them cleaning out their burrows in late October and early November. Whether they do any underground remodeling of burrows and plugged tunnels in winter is unknown. The work they do during the active season, however, results in great soil movement and soil modification.

House-cleaning job. Prairie dogs sometimes clean out galleries that have been used for toilet purposes.

In bringing earth to the surface they hasten its breakdown by weathering. Lower soil layers are mixed with upper soil layers. Organic matter, including clipped roots, grass leaves, feces, urine, and insect remains, are also added to the soil. The burrows themselves permit penetration of water and aeration of soils. Thus, the many generations of prairie dogs living in the same locality deepen the soil and add to its productivity.

Koford in his review of the literature on rodent-soil relationships wrote that in northern Colorado an average prairie dog mound is made up of about 3 cubic feet of soil. On the basis of twenty-five burrows per acre he computed the weight of the soil in mounds to be over 3 tons. He also calculated the volume of soil excavated from burrows of known length, described by other workers, using an assumed diameter of 5 inches and a soil weight of 80 pounds per cubic foot. These computations gave an estimated volume of 4 tons of earth raised from the twenty-five surface holes per acre.

A greater effect made by prairie dogs and badgers on soil was found by James Thorn, who stated that the activities of these animals actually altered the original soil from silt loam to loam. The weight of one mound, 24 feet in diameter, was computed at 22,360 pounds. The average weight of mounds was 3,770 pounds, and the weight of soil excavated by the

By late September the young adult prairie dog has developed a sense of caution.

combined activities of prairie dogs and badgers was estimated at 32.5 tons per acre.

The burrowing activity of rodents improves soil fertility by adding calcium, magnesium, and other salts to surface soil layers. Loosened soil also absorbs water more readily than soil compacted by the trampling of large grazing animals. In this respect, prairie dogs probably counteracted much of the hardening of surface soil done by the feet of countless bison.

Considerable quantities of soil and grass are scraped from the surface in the vicinity of prairie dog mounds. Some of this is incorporated into the mound to form a sort of adobe which hardens and makes the mound almost indestructible. This mixture prevents erosion of the crater rim, which acts as a dyke when violent rainstorms flood the area surrounding the mounds.

The quantities of soil brought up from the earth by prairie dogs are indicative of the great labor expended underground. Very little is known about the subterranean doings of these animals. No one has yet devised a simple method which will permit observation of prairie dogs in their tunnels.

It might be possible to monitor the movements of prairie dogs underground by means of radio signal locator equipment. To my knowledge no one has attempted this. Porcupines and birds have been followed successfully with radio equipment, and ants have been bugged underground with radioactive tracers. Surely a similar study of prairie dog underground movements could be done to reveal many of their presently unknown activities.

Tileston observed that adult white-tailed prairie dogs spent 50 per cent of their day inside their burrows. Since they are diurnal animals, they spend 100 per cent of their night below ground. How much of their underground time is spent in sleeping, digging, nest construction, and other activities? Do they sleep all night? Do they indulge in other activities such as mating? And how far do prairie dogs retreat into their tunnels when predators make them dive to safety? No one knows.

As autumn begins its transition into winter, the prairie dogs spend more of their time below ground, devoting less time to feeding, grooming, basking in the sun, and defending the coterie territory. Periods of inclement weather reduce their activity. Wind and dust storms drive the animals to their burrows. Occasional snowstorms in autumn plug the burrow entrances with snow, but these are opened when the weather moderates and tracks appear between burrows and at the edges of clear spaces where the prairie dogs feed during warm periods of the day.

The final food harvest for the white-tailed adults in the mountains comes as early as August. Forage is still lush and green, and fat is accumulated in time for the long quiescent period of eight months or more underground. The juveniles, however, remain active into October and are able to reap the nutritious crop of seeds produced by late-season grasses that mature a few weeks before the prairie dog world is covered with snow.

In autumn on the plains, rains may cause the germination of winter annuals such as cheat-grass brome. The nutritious seedlings of these plants are eagerly sought by the black-tailed prairie dogs. These green winter foods, in combination with the seasonal sprouts of four-wing saltbush, semiherbaceous sages, and prickly-pear stems, provide the dietary variety and vitamin supplements necessary for the prairie dogs' winter preparations.

The close of autumn terminates many accomplishments and processes in prairie dog town. Stability of populations and establishment of territorial boundaries have been achieved through separation of adults and young, through expansion of the town limits, and through migration. The autumnal molt has been completed, and prairie dogs now have thicker, longer fur. They have dug permanent burrows. Some hawks and eagles have migrated, although coyotes, badgers, ferrets, and other predators still remain.

Dog town becomes a quieter place as autumn merges into winter. Many of the summer birds have gone southward, but magpies, crows, and rabbits are still there and new resident birds arrive from the north, including the longspurs and juncos. The grasshoppers and other insects have perished with the frosts, and the ground squirrels, lizards, toads, and box turtles have entered their deep hibernating sleep.

And yet, not all is quiet. The prairie dogs come above ground from time to time, as they do all through the winter. Even when the blizzards of January are blowing, their internal physiology will be changing in preparation for the mating season soon to follow. In only a few months the great activity of prairie dog town will burst forth again with the advent of another spring.

A relaxed prairie dog on a crater mound. Note the nose marks around the tunnel entrance.

Prairie dog in winter in North Dakota. (National Park Service)

Winter

ON THE PLAINS, much of the prairie dog's winter is snowless. Blizzards come and go. Periodically the raw cold abates and the subtle pastels of cured grasses and dried herbs are visible under blue skies and brilliant sunshine. The hoarfrost that coats the prairies and the lingering snow that persists around their mounds does not deter the prairie dogs on pleasant days, and they emerge into the world of winter finches, pipits, juncos, and longspurs that harvest the autumn seeds.

In the foothills and in the level meadows at middle elevations of the

Prairie dogs are active in winter when snow is on the ground. (Park and Recreation Commission, Lubbock, Texas)

mountains, the winter winds sweep the grasslands bare. There on pleasant days the white-tailed prairie dogs step out and begin their feeding and travels between mounds. On the Laramie Plains east of the Snowy Range in southern Wyoming, I have seen them scurrying about in late January and early February, impelled to early preparation for the greater family activity to come in spring.

In the higher mountain valleys and parks, ten thousand feet or more in elevation, prairie dog country remains snowbound and winter sleep continues. Deep in their underground chambers, prairie dogs are free of enemies. The fat they accumulated in the previous summer and autumn sustains their life until the weather frees them in March, in April, or even as late as May.

On the plains, in the absence of inclement weather, a few black-tailed prairie dogs are usually above ground from October through December. The peak of activity comes about midday and may last for an hour or two. Most of their time is spent in feeding. Males are more active than females in this season. All the animals of a colony never appear above ground together on any given day or period of days. Investigators have surmised from this that prairie dogs become dormant for short periods and then resume activity.

In January and February, when blizzards and intense cold are not upon the land, the black-tailed prairie dogs enter a period of pre-breeding activity. Feeding does not appear to be important. But the amount of grooming, kissing, and olfactory examination increases.

Females object sometimes to the attentions of the males and run to their burrows when pursued. Occasionally there are fights between the sexes at the burrow entrances, and then the males return to their feeding or explore their territories. Invasions by males from other coteries are common, and the antagonism continues for several weeks.

The annual breeding season of the prairie dog comes early, although it varies according to weather conditions and geographic location. In Texas and Oklahoma, mating is common in late January and February. In

Snow lingers on the ground when prairie dogs appear in early spring. (National Park Service)

Montana and the Dakotas it may not occur until March. The annual breeding period is limited to about two or three weeks and is the culmination of a reproductive cycle influenced by various environmental and physiological factors. Many of the phenomena that precede full sexual development of males and females still are not thoroughly understood. Functional development of the reproductive systems of male black-tailed prairie dogs begins in late autumn and reaches its height generally in February. Gradually the reproductive glands increase in size and the male is able to impregnate the female for a period of four or five weeks, beginning as a rule in late January. Early in March the reproductive organs return to their quiescent state, and the males are no longer capable of mating.

Female prairie dogs generally show the first signs of ovarian activity in December. By late January the uterus grows and other physiological changes make the females receptive to mating in January and February. After pregnancy, the reproductive organs of the females subside into an inactive state.

Few people have witnessed the copulation of prairie dogs, since encounters between the sexes during the mating season often result in fights where the female repels the male at the burrow entrance. The receptivity period of the female is so short that observation of copulation is almost impossible. Also, it is probable that successful mating occurs primarily in the burrows. When the gestation period begins, the females vigorously defend their nesting burrows. They also intensify their food-gathering efforts. Winter feeding, however, even during the time of pregnancy, may be sporadic among prairie dogs.

Only during feeding time in winter are prairie dogs vulnerable to predation by eagles, bobcats, and coyotes; since the prairie dogs spend much of their winter underground they are less available to predators than at other seasons. Their open-air visits are also of short duration, and they do not wander far from the home burrows. Still, they have fierce enemies that can cause trouble in dog town.

Chipmunks normally dig their own burrows, but use prairie dog burrows for escape from enemies.

Black-footed ferrets and badgers remain active during the winter. The ferrets are so rare, however, that they cannot be considered effective winter enemies. Badgers are occasionally active in dog towns when other prey, such as mice and cottontail rabbits, is scarce. Most badger work, however, occurs in late summer in new shallow burrows at the edges of towns.

Coyotes frequent prairie dog towns in winter and occasionally catch an unwary animal that wanders too far from its burrow. There are not as many prairie dog eyes to watch for danger in winter, and this may contribute to the coyote's success in hunting.

I have seen coyotes in dog towns during winter, but they were not stalking prairie dogs. Instead, they seemed to be searching for mice, because they spent considerable time sniffing and digging into grass clumps. They also carefully examined the "forms" or open-air resting places used by cottontails for hiding. In winter, in spite of the few animals above ground at any one time, the prairie dogs are able to guard against four-footed predators with considerable success since their towns there are relatively free of tall plants and visibility is good over long distances.

Animals that hibernate in dog towns are not winter enemies, and few of them cause any great inconvenience for the prairie dogs. Some of

Wood rats also use prairie dog tunnels for refuge when enemies appear.

these have already been mentioned: snakes, toads, box turtles, lizards, salamanders, insects, and ground squirrels. Numerous adult spiders live in prairie dog burrows as well as in crevices in the ground and under stones. Occasionally, the young of wolf spiders hibernate in animal dens and mature the following summer. These are the long-legged spiders that run rapidly over the ground and through grass in search of insect prey.

Rattlesnakes are notorious for hibernating in prairie dog towns. The rattlers are most numerous around the burrows during autumn migration from their summer hunting grounds and in spring when they sun themselves for many days before departing for other haunts. Rattlers often gather in large numbers when the temperature begins to fall after a period of mild weather.

Koford has cited the record of C. B. Perkins, who collected 863 rattlesnakes from three prairie dog towns near Platteville, Colorado. I once helped in the eradication of 63 rattlesnakes outside a rock den near Grover, Colorado. We killed these snakes because they were a menace to young lambs in a nearby pasture and to school children, who had to walk along a road traversed by snakes in their spring migration. There were prairie dog towns in the vicinity, but the snakes seemed to prefer the rock outcrop, with its many holes and fissures, for their winter sleep.

Although striped skunks are abroad in winter, they den up occasionally during spells of severe weather. Sometimes several skunks will use a single abandoned prairie dog burrow. The fat they have accumulated by eating mice and insects in autumn allows them to curl up and remain inactive for several weeks, although they seldom stay for more than a month at a time. Moderate weather brings them out again. Since they search for partners and mate as early as mid-February, one may see their tracks in dog town long before the winter snow has thawed.

Parasitic fleas live in dog town through the winter and may cause widespread disease among rodents in summer. The fleas that parasitize prairie dogs are carriers of sylvatic or rodent plague. The principal fleas that transmit plague are *Opisocrostis hirsutus* and *O. tuberculatus cynomuris*. Other fleas live on prairie dogs, including *Pulex irritans* and *Leptopsylla segnis*. The prairie dogs have such dense hair in winter that they are efficient reservoirs for disease-carrying fleas.

Epizootic, or large scale, outbreaks of sylvatic plague among prairie dogs have been observed in various places in recent years. These have resulted in scare articles in newspapers and magazines, in extensive studies by public health agencies, and in justifications for massive extermination campaigns by government rodent control experts. As usual, the control efforts have been too late and therefore have been directed toward the wrong animals.

The plague bacillus, *Pasteurella pestris*, which causes sylvatic plague in ground squirrels, may be harbored by mice, cottontails, marmots, and other rodents and is presumed by the best authorities to have been brought from the Orient by infested rats. The first recognized case of human plague in the United States was in San Francisco in 1900. According to Dean H. Ecke and Clifford W. Johnson (1952), a minor epidemic followed, with 121 cases and 113 deaths. A second outbreak among humans occurred in 1907-1908, with 160 cases and 78 deaths.

The Oriental rats that brought the plague probably infected the local rats, and they, in turn, passed it on to the native ground squirrels. From the California ground squirrels the plague spread to rodent populations in the interior of the United States. At the same time, the U.S. Fish and Wildlife Service mounted strict eradication programs against prairie dogs, particularly in Colorado. No attempt was made to control other native rodent carriers of the plague. The rats are still with us.

In Park County, Colorado, sylvatic plague nearly wiped out Gunnison's prairie dogs from approximately 627,000 acres in about four years. Wyoming ground squirrels, deer mice, and meadow mice also suffered high mortality from the disease. Meadow mice are plague positive and have a high flea index. Coyotes are able to transport fleas over large areas since they can travel fifteen or more miles a day. A good question then is: "Which animal brought the disease that decimated the Colorado prairie dogs?" Ecke and Johnson state that in one case a rancher drove 250 miles from his home to obtain diseased animals. Thus, plague epizootics may make abnormal jumps over great distances through human as well as animal agency.

Officials of the U.S. Public Health Service say bubonic plague occurs in about two people per year in the United States and is not a cause for alarm. Health officials warn that persons in remote areas should avoid handling chipmunks, rabbits, squirrels, rats, and other rodents, especially if the animals appear to be sick or if they are dead. The few cases of bubonic plague reported in recent years in the United States, however, appear to have been connected with animals other than prairie dogs.

Vaccinations against plague are now available. Human cases can also be treated effectively with streptomycin, sulfonamides, or combinations of tetracycline antibiotics. Dr. Robert R. Lechleitner, Associate Professor of Zoology at Colorado State University, who has made many studies

PRAIRIE DOGS ARE GROUND SQUIRRELS   THEY BARK LIKE DOGS

PRAIRIE DOG TOWN

FLOOD DYKE & WATCHTOWER
FOOD & MOISTURE SUPPLY

CHOOSING A SITE

HOME
BUILDING

KICKING OUT DIRT

Remarkable social animals, they live together in permanent 'towns'. Numerous mounds mark burrow entrances. 'Dogs' eat the grass and scoop up soil for their mounds making the townsite almost barren.

LISTENING POST

TOILET

DRY ROOM
used when chamber is wet

PUSHING OUT DIRT   BULLDOZING   PACKING DIRT   TAKING IT EASY   CHAMBER

Prairie dogs are wild animals. Watch them from a safe distance – they can bite ! Some may carry disease. Wild animals need wild food so please don't feed them. Dependent on your handouts, they lose their natural ability to survive the long winter.

Signs describing prairie dog activities are found in recreation areas. This one is at Devil's Tower National Monument, Wyoming.

of prairie dogs, stated, "It is unlikely that a human will contract bubonic plague from a prairie dog without handling the animal."

While I fondled his roly-poly eight-year-old prairie dog, Fum—the survivor of three others he called, Fe, Fi, and Fo—Dr. Lechleitner told me he believes prairie dogs are among our best barometers of plague and should be preserved for that reason alone. They are easily observed. When an epizootic of plague starts among rodents, it can be quickly detected by watching prairie dogs.

Dr. Lechleitner also believes that badgers may develop antibodies against plague. At least, badgers seem to have survived in areas where various rodents have been infected with the disease. Similarly four of twenty-four monkeys exposed to killing doses of plague organisms at the Naval Biological Laboratory in California recovered and possibly became carriers.

Prairie dogs do not appear to be susceptible to many of the diseases common to those predatory animals that eat a large variety of prey. Their vegetarian habits may help them avoid the large numbers of parasites they might otherwise acquire if they were pronounced meat eaters. Koford, writing of the black-tailed prairie dogs, also suggested that "the separation of dog towns as discrete units, with little interchange of dogs between them, has protective survival value against the spread of sweeping epizootics such as afflicted the Gunnison prairie dog, a less colonial species."

Little has been written about the survival of individual prairie dog towns. Prairie dogs themselves have survived for thousands of years. The stability of their environment, especially on the prairie, which has remained essentially unchanged since the Ice Age, has no doubt contributed to their success as a distinctive group of rodents, as has their social organization, before human interference changed their relationships with nature. Fluctuations in food supplies from year to year undoubtedly caused changes in the coterie organization through migration and mortality from predators. The advantages of living together, coupled with their defense warning system, however, preserved established communities from all enemies. Emigration also resulted in interbreeding of prairie dogs with other population groups and genetic variability which kept the species vigorous. Furthermore, the habit of making a deep burrow system contributed to the permanence of prairie dog territory.

The burrow systems enable prairie dogs to endure severe winters that are sometimes catastrophic to animals that must live above ground. A study in the files of the National Park Service which I examined at the Theodore Roosevelt National Memorial Park indicates that no prairie dog town has been "lost" since 1947. A few towns became uninhabited for a time but were later reinhabited. In this study, aerial photos were used to designate town locations and were planimetered by passing a tracer around the boundary lines on the photos to determine the sizes of the towns.

There were three towns in 1947; one in 1951; fourteen in 1953; nine in 1956; eight in 1957; nineteen in 1962-1963; and eighteen in 1964-1965. I found a similar situation at the Devil's Tower National Monument in Wyoming. The ranger said, "The towns dry up on one side and bulge out somewhere else."

The longest period of occupation I know is in a foothill town in Larimer County, Colorado. I first saw it in 1936 and went back there each spring over a period of many years to see if the prairie dogs had survived the winter. The rancher who owned the place told me when I first saw the colony that it had been there for many years. It was still there when I visited it in 1969. Populations and boundaries had fluctuated through the years, but the town apparently has been in that same vicinity for more than half a century.

Typical prairie dog grassland in the badlands of South Dakota.

Prairie dogs at Devil's Tower National Monument, Wyoming.

Prairie Dogs and Men

No one knows the exact time prairie dogs first inhabited the prairie. The prairie itself had its real beginning in the Cenozoic era, known as the age of mammals. Monroe D. Bryant has suggested that the prairie dogs became distinct from primitive squirrel ancestors early in Miocene times and separated from other genera of ground squirrels in the Pliocene era over a period of some twenty-five million years.

Fossils of prairie dogs have been found in late Pleistocene deposits, along with the skeletal remains of a Pleistocene horse. Claude W. Hibbard has suggested that prairie dogs have not changed to any great extent in the last million years, since fossil specimens show characteristics similar to those of our modern black-tailed prairie dogs.

Prairie dogs lived on the grasslands through the Ice Age and undoubtedly changed their distribution with the four major advances of glacial ice over the northern part of the continent. They lived with the bison, pronghorns, deer, elk, bears, wolves, and other plains animals that existed in countless thousands on the original prairie. According to James B. Griffin, not until some sixteen to twenty thousand years ago, when the Bering land bridge appeared, were men able to come across from Asia and enter the prairie dog's world.

These first men, the ancestors of our modern Indians, were hunters who used flint tools in their culture, which involved the use of a number of plants and animals for food, clothing, magical charms, and ornaments.

121

These primitive people ate animals of the grasslands, including the prairie dogs.

Archaeological studies have indicated that prairie dogs were a source of food for prehistoric man, especially when bison and other big game animals were scarce. Waldo R. Wedel testified that caves of great antiquity near Kenton, Oklahoma, contained bones of various animals and ears of corn stored in a bag made of prairie dog skins. In recent times, the Navajo Indians considered prairie dogs to be a delicacy until white men poisoned the prairie dogs in the Indians' territory.

Many of the early travelers across the plans were impressed by the burrowing activities of rodents and made records of them in their journals. John C. Fremont, for example, who marched by way of the Santa Fe Trail in 1842, recorded his first sighting of prairie dogs and bison. Lieutenant James W. Abert, who traveled westward from Fort Leavenworth in 1845, observed that pocket gophers were associated with tall grasses and prairie dogs with short grasses.

Before these records were made, Edwin James, the botanist for the Stephen H. Long expedition of 1820, wrote descriptions of prairie dog towns in what is now Nebraska and Colorado. Other detailed descriptions, listed by James C. Malin, were made by Captain R. B. Marcy "on the southern Great Plains in 1849, 1852, and 1854, especially the Red River report of 1852 which included the valley of the South Fork, a stream which the Comanches called Prairie Dog Town River."

With the coming of American "civilization," wolves, coyotes, badgers, and prairie dogs presented serious economic problems to Western stockmen. In spite of the fact that grazing animals had lived on the plains for ten thousand years without obliterating the grass, prairie dogs were accused of destroying plant life "root and branch." Vernon Bailey, in his *Biological Survey of Texas,* published in 1905, estimated the number of prairie dogs in that state in 1901 at 800 million and reported that these would require as much grass as 3,125,000 cattle. Such estimates marked the beginning of extensive studies published in bulletins of agricultural

Sheep, when poorly managed, overgraze desert grasslands. If prairie dogs are present, they are forced to graze on saltbush, sagebrush, and other shrubs.

experiment stations and in livestock magazines concerning the destructiveness and control of prairie dogs.

The coming of the longhorns from the south and the conquest of the prairie by cattle and plows from the east made the slaughter of prairie dogs and other "varmints" inevitable. Because of their alleged direct competition with livestock and because of their depredations on cultivated crops, prairie dogs have for a hundred years been relentlessly persecuted by federal, state, and private interests. C. Hart Merriam provoked interest in this destruction by publication of "The Prairie Dog of the Great Plains" in the *Yearbook of Agriculture* for 1901.

In the nearly seventy years since Merriam's study was made, an amazing number of authors have cited his accounts of the millions of prairie dogs in Texas and the millions of dollars' worth of forage killed annually. But the writers have generally ignored Merriam's explanation of how the coming of the white man favored the multiplication of prairie dogs: by decreasing their natural enemies, by increasing the prairie dogs' food supply by growing crops, and by destruction of the tall grasses on which prairie dogs fed.

With the coming of the white man, prairie dogs became "pests" because of the wholesale slaughter of their predators—badgers, coyotes, bobcats, weasels, hawks, eagles, and snakes. At the same time prairie dogs and other rodents were blamed for destroying ranges rather than farmers' recognizing overgrazed ranges as a symptom of poor livestock management. Evidence has been furnished by many investigators, including Richard M. Bond, Walter P. Taylor and W. B. Davis, Ben Osborn and Phillip F. Allan, and J. J. Norris, which indicates that prairie dogs tend to be most numerous on ranges depleted by livestock overgrazing.

Tim W. Clark has pointed out that under certain conditions rodents *speed* the recovery of deteriorated ranges. Many rodents feed mainly on annual forbs and other plants typical of early stages of plant succession, thus favoring the increase of grasses and other livestock forage plants. Koford wrote that if man does not alter the grassland, it is improbable that prairie dogs alone will reduce the range vegetation below the stage where short grasses are dominant.

The history of prairie dog control by poisoning and bounty payments has been a long one. C. Hart Merriam, in the *Yearbook of Agriculture* for 1901, listed cyanide of potassium and strychnine as efficient killers. The cyanide was placed in prunes and raisins which were sometimes mixed with grain poisoned with strychnine and disguised with molasses flavored with oil of anise. Also, grain soaked with strychnine, mixed with corn meal, and made into pellets was scattered about the holes.

Bisulphide of carbon was used as a fumigant, but the mechanical devices needed to pump the fumes into the ground often did not work. A more simple method consisted in pouring a tablespoonful of the volatile liquid on a lump of horse manure or a corncob which was dropped into the burrow, the mouth of which was then closed. (In this modern age of jeeps and tractors, Merriam's statement about horse

Pet prairie dog enjoys corn on the cob.

manure, that it costs nothing and is always at hand, is no longer true.)

Since 1900 the history of prairie dog "control" has been one of ever increasing efficiency in methods of killing. Numerous state laws were enacted, including ones that permitted a majority of landowners in a control district to force all property holders to share in the cost of rodent poisoning. These laws took many forms.

The 1927 law of North Dakota, for example, stated: "The County Commissioners shall, upon the petition of not less than 20 per cent of the total number of votes cast in the last election, offer a bounty or reward for each gopher, rabbit, crow, and prairie dog destroyed during the year." The 1945 legislature allowed the County Commissioners to levy a tax of one half mill on all real estate to create a bounty fund for "pests," which included prairie dogs.

Recently, bounty payments have had little impact on prairie dog control, since payment of the bounty requires that some part of the

125

animal be produced as evidence of kill. The newer chemicals are so efficient that many rodents die underground and their bodies are not available to substantiate proof of eradication.

One of the effective poisons was thallium sulfate, introduced about 1928. With the aid of federal funds and labor from Civilian Conservation Corps, Works Progress Administration, and Emergency Conservation Work projects, more than one million acres of prairie dog towns in Colorado were treated with this substance.

In 1947, Compound 1080 (sodium fluoracetate), one of the most deadly animal poisons ever developed, was applied to 1,210,000 acres in Colorado under the supervision of the U.S. Fish and Wildlife Service. The "experts" here and elsewhere made little or no attempt to ascertain the effects of 1080 on mammals and birds that fed on the carcasses of the poisoned rodents. But as Koford reported: "Some of the effects on the community do not appear until weeks, months, or even years after poisoning. It is not certain that continuous widespread poisoning is doing more good than harm, in the long run, or that the apparent economic benefits of poisoning are worth the cost in materials, labor, and administration."

John Madson, in a report in *Audubon* on the status of the prairie dog and the black-footed ferret, suggested that the motivation for mass slaughter of prairie dogs comes from "the constant agitation and proselytizing of federal rodent control officers." The pressure for extermination emanates not from Washington, D.C., but from local field men who are interested in job continuance and from western politicians who believe they have the best interests of landowners in mind.

Not all landowners go along with the exterminators, as Madson pointed out in his report. In my own recent travels of more than 12,000 miles in nine "prairie dog" states, I met many ranchers who enjoyed seeing a few prairie dogs and who were intolerant of any control by subsidized crews, surreptitious or otherwise. Federal conservationists, especially those in the National Parks, looked askance at the control work but were hesitant to criticize programs being carried out by branches of their own department.

State wildlife specialists in Montana, North Dakota, South Dakota, and Nebraska were reluctant to direct me to prairie dog towns in their areas of jurisdiction until I gave them assurance I was not a federal agent seeking to locate colonies for extermination. It was accepted among these men that prairie dogs do considerable damage in local areas, but they wanted no program that would destroy the total animal ecology now so rapidly vanishing from the prairie.

A considerable number of ranchers allow "varmint" hunting in their prairie dog towns. Some charge a fee for this target practice; others regulate the number of animals that can be killed in order to maintain a continuous supply.

Rodent hunters, however, exert only minor control over prairie dog populations. Ronald E. Smith stated that "if the hunters had been more accurate and the prairie dogs less prolific and less agile, the millions of rounds of ammunition expended in their direction would long ago have placed the prairie dog in the present position of the dodo bird."

I personally can testify to the wariness that prairie dogs develop when they are persistently harassed by snipers and ardent varminters. Recently, for example, in a remote area in extreme northwest Utah, I drove my truck for several miles over hazardous roads to photograph white-tailed prairie dogs in a town that contained several hundred animals. I had hoped the shooters had overlooked the prairie dogs in this isolated area, but when I arrived, the dogs disappeared almost immediately, even those at measured distances of three to four hundred yards. Although I camped overnight at the edge of the town and waited until noon of the following day, only six dogs were visible, even through binoculars. I found cartridge cases of 22-250 Remington on the ground, indicating long-range shooting of up to possibly four hundred yards.

Prairie dog target shooters generally use flat trajectory ammunition with plenty of zip. Some load their own ammunition for use at short

Prairie dogs make popular zoo animals. (Colorado Game, Fish and Parks Department)

range, 150 yards or so; medium range, to 250 yards; and long range, 300 yards and up. At the longer ranges a scope sight, up to a magnification of twelve times, is a necessity. The calibers used vary all the way from .22 rimfire through .220 Swift, 270, to 30-06 or larger. Opinions regarding weights of bullets, trajectory, and the problem of windage — the wind nearly always blows in prairie dog country — are almost as numerous as the varminters themselves.

In spite of all the attention men have given prairie dogs — as targets to shoot at, pests to be poisoned, and as ecological components of the environment — relatively little information is available on the social structure of their colonies or on their place in nature. The Zuni prairie dog, Gunnison's prairie dog, and the Utah prairie dog are practically extinct. Only recently have detailed comparison studies of white-tailed and black-tailed prairie dog habits been made, such as the one by Tileston and Lechleitner published in 1966.

Man is to blame for much of the conflict between prairie dogs and himself. As a result of his tinkering with nature and his indiscriminate killing of both plants and animals with plows, chemicals, guns, and overgrazing, he has changed the ecological functioning of the landscape. If more effort were spent in investigating how animals live and in learning the basic reasons why certain species acquire pest status, man might be able to better utilize the remaining grasslands. Some of his "pests" might even prove to be friends.

Many facts about the prairie dog have been learned by people who have reared them in captivity or made friends with them in nature. When treated kindly, they become delightful and confiding pets.

A report by Stanley P. Young in the *Journal of Mammalogy* stated that Lieutenant James Abert, while stationed at Fort Bent near the Arkansas River in the late 1840s, mentioned that caged prairie dogs were kept as pets behind the high adobe walls of the fort. Young himself kept two prairie dogs as pets. One of these was a male Zuni prairie dog that lived in his kitchen, dining room, garage, and basement for eight and one half years. The other was a black-tailed prairie dog from southwestern Oklahoma. This one, named Abigail, also lived with Young for eight and one half years. Neither animal was given water to drink, but they ate almost any kind of food, including green vegetables, raw carrots, cabbage, clover, orange pulp, and salted peanuts.

Even though the two animals were of different species they lived peacefully together. They kept a mound of earth in a caged runway in repair. Both came when called and liked to be scratched under the chin. Between May and October they put on fat until they weighed nearly four pounds.

The male became dormant in late November when the first heavy frosts set in. He slept curled in a ball with his head tucked into his body fur a short distance above his hind legs. He became active in February or early March. The female, on the other hand, scarcely slept more than four days at a time. She was ready to breed after late April. But since the male was ready to breed in early March, no young dogs were produced.

Lorene Squire, a famous wildlife photographer, had a pet prairie dog called Cutie that learned his name and would come when called, if he wanted to. He was an inquisitive animal and could open a door by sticking a paw in the crack and pulling. He chewed up a fur coat, shredded

129

a curtain, and tore up magazines. He investigated rats, dueled with them, and killed one. He played with a fox terrier, but when a cat stalked him, he jumped first and bit the cat on the leg. When angry he growled and chattered his teeth.

The telephone bell always made him bark, which was done with paws folded over his stomach. The bark jerked his tail and he made a funny little bow—clear to the floor and back again. He often barked when eating.

E. C. Cates in Montana owned a young male black-tailed prairie dog, named Keogh in honor of Fort Keogh, that grew up to be an intelligent, responsive pet. At the time of capture he had not been weaned, but he soon graduated from bread and milk to green grass, corn, wheat, barley, rye, and canned sweet potatoes. He drank water very sparingly and lapped it while keeping his tongue in his mouth, which was submerged. He played with a collie dog and showed no fear of cats. He was always suspicious of sudden noises or quick movements. When a bird flew overhead, he fled to his box.

Keogh began digging holes in the lawn after his first month in captivity. These were no more than six or eight inches deep. In August he dug burrows about three feet in depth. He would have gone farther, but a small chain attached to his collar kept him from continuing down. When taken to prairie dog towns he usually inspected several burrows, then selected one and cleaned it out in true prairie dog fashion. He was accidentally poisoned in the poison-mixing room at the college in Bozeman.

At the Prairie Homestead managed by Keith and Dorothy Crew, near Interior, South Dakota, white prairie dogs and abundant black-tailed dogs were so tame that they ate from the Crew children's hands. If the children did not give them enough food, the prairie dogs would bite their fingers. Because of this Dorothy told me her husband had to take one of the animals to a native colony. When the children learned about this, they cried until the pet was brought back.

Prairie dogs at roadside eating potato chips fed to them by tourists.

Young prairie dogs are live-trapped for scientific studies. They are easy to raise in the laboratory.

Even wild prairie dogs become tame when they associate with people. The prairie dogs at the Devil's Tower National Monument have a habit of coming regularly to the roadside, there to be fed peanuts and potato chips by the tourists. These unnatural foods are detrimental to the prairie dogs' systems because they often become dependent upon them and can die from the lack of nourishment.

Capturing prairie dogs, especially the young ones, for pets or for scientific purposes presents no particular problem. My barber tells me he used to catch prairie dogs in Montana with a string looped around the hole in the mound. Live animal traps work well if they are baited with barley or oats. Gloves should be used when handling the older animals, since they may bite fiercely.

Live traps are commonly used by scientists when they need prairie dogs for reproductive cycle studies or when they require captive laboratory colonies for investigation of growth rates and feeding habits. Laboratory studies are also made for the detection of internal parasites

132

and disease organisms. Prairie dogs are often live-trapped for release in other areas, so that their behavior in establishing new colonies can be studied.

One of the earliest attempts at transplanting prairie dogs was described by C. Hart Merriam:

> In 1890–1892, one or two pairs of prairie dogs were introduced into Nantucket, where, for several years, they increased slowly and were regarded with interest. After a few years, however, they grew so numerous and spread so rapidly that the inhabitants became greatly alarmed and feared the animals would overrun the whole island. Mr. Outram Bangs wrote in December, 1899, that when on a visit to the island during the summer and fall of the same year he counted 200 prairie dogs visible at one time in one colony, and states that three or four such colonies existed, besides many scattering pairs and small colonies.

At a town meeting, therefore, $350 was appropriated to buy poison and the prairie dogs were subsequently eliminated. Merriam did not report how the prairie dogs were captured in the first place.

Flooding has been used by farmers to oust prairie dogs from their holes. This is done by turning irrigation water into a town built on level ground. The practice is not always successful, since some of the prairie dogs survive in air chambers built into their tunnel system.

Anthony and Foreman used flooding to capture prairie dogs for a laboratory study of their reproductive cycles. In the Wichita Mountains Wildlife Refuge near Cache, Oklahoma, they filled the burrows with water from fire-fighting trucks. The dogs were caught with either gloved hands, screen-mesh cones, or a wet sack.

In an attempt to establish prairie dog colonies through releases of wild-trapped animals in North Dakota, Arthur W. Adams used an 1,800-gallon water truck which pumped water into the holes at about 150 gallons per minute. "Some holes filled quickly, most required about five minutes of pumping to fill, and some were seemingly impossible to fill."

Prairie dogs in parks and zoos generally are tame and make excellent photographic subjects.

The adult prairie dogs were snared with landing nets. The young were picked out of the holes when they floated to the surface.

A different, but effective, method of capturing young prairie dogs was used by Warren Garst. A one-inch slice from a stick of dynamite was inserted in an auger hole directly above the tunnel where young animals had previously appeared. Electric detonator wires radiated fifty to a hundred yards from the observer's station to selected mounds. When the young were above ground the dynamite was detonated to collapse the hole. Since the juvenile prairie dogs were unfamiliar with other escape routes, they milled around the home burrow and were easily picked up.

Prairie dogs are frequently captured for zoos and recreation areas, where they become major attractions for children and adults. One of the most famous city-maintained prairie dog towns is in Lubbock, Texas, a seven-acre dog town in Mackenzie State Park, within the city limits. Mr. and Mrs. K. N. Clapp originated the idea, and the dog town was established from two burrows of the original colony in 1932.

134

The city of Lubbock protects these prairie dogs. There is a $500 fine for molesting them. Mr. A. C. Hamilton, Director of Parks and Recreation, informed me that the dog town is well stocked and thriving. The Chamber of Commerce points out that more than a million people come each year to see it.

In 1968 Boulder, Colorado, had three prairie dog towns within the city limits. One town was at the edge of the campus of the University of Colorado. As I watched them in their plot of a few acres, cars were speeding by on a four-lane highway on one side; students were coming and going on campus on the other.

Another town was surrounded by houses and apartment buildings. The third was in a vacant lot. The little animals, living on their restricted remnants of prairie, were fenced in by civilization and had no place to go. They could not expand their towns or segregate their society into family groups and wards, as they do on the open prairie. They seemed dispirited and did not bark when I moved among them.

In 1966 a colony of prairie dogs took up residence in Elmer Thomas Park on a few acres of grass located behind the Museum of the Great Plains and the McMahon Auditorium in Lawton, Oklahoma. The colony prospered, grew to more than sixty individuals, and became a unique attraction. The trustees of the Great Plains Historical Association asked the city council of Lawton to pass an ordinance designed to protect and preserve the dog town, and this was finally done. Now there are about two hundred prairie dogs directly behind the museum, and a smaller town of some forty to fifty dogs is located directly east of the museum.

Prairie dogs also have been used for commercial interests. For example, the Ranch Store in Kadoka, South Dakota, advertised as the gateway to the Badlands, has a natural prairie dog town nearby, fenced and protected with "Keep Out" signs. A much larger prairie dog town, also privately owned, adjoins the protected one. I walked through and found not only prairie dogs but burrowing owls and rattlesnakes.

In Kadoka also, advertised for many miles along the highways, is "The

Author and "World's Largest Prairie Dog" at Kadoka, South Dakota.

World's Largest Prairie Dog," a realistic statue of a prairie dog, about twenty feet high.

The largest towns of prairie dogs, where one may see and study them at leisure, are in the national parks and national monuments in the Dakotas and at Devil's Tower National Monument, Wyoming. Prairie dogs are also numerous in Custer State Park and Wind Cave National Monument in the Black Hills, South Dakota. These are ideal places for

136

prairie dog photography, because highways go right through some of the towns and the prairie dogs are not particularly afraid of people.

In a park where they are relatively tame, shooting pictures of prairie dogs is not difficult. They are above ground only in daytime, when the light is generally good. With high-speed black and white film, it is generally possible to hand hold a camera with a moderate length telephoto lens, use a shutter speed of 1/1000 of a second, and get sharp pictures free of blur and movement. Even with ultra-slow color film it is possible to get color slides at 1/500 of a second at f/4 in bright sunlight.

If you want to give your friends a complete picture of prairie dog life, do not be stingy with film. Be sure to shoot pictures of prairie dog adults and young on their mounds. Also, try to get shots of them eating, grooming, kissing, and digging. Maybe, if you are lucky, you can catch one in the act of nose tamping after a rainstorm or happen upon one when it is giving the territorial or "let's eat" call.

Professional students of prairie dogs sometimes use blinds for wildlife photography. These are made of burlap, canvas, or other materials, or are simply umbrella tents to which the prairie dogs grow accustomed in time. I frequently photograph prairie dogs from my truck camper, which has windows that can be opened on three sides.

Some of my most interesting pictures, however, have been taken by stalking with the stealth of a great blue heron approaching a frog in a lily pond. I move inch by inch when a prairie dog is eating, and stop when he looks up. It is hard on leg muscles, but in this way I have been able to come as near as fifteen feet to adult animals. This is close enough for a 135-mm. or 150-mm. lens. Young prairie dogs can sometimes be stalked to within three or four feet by constantly looking through the view finder and gradually stooping or squatting, so as to present a direct forward appearance. If you try to walk up slowly without stooping as you go, your body appears to grow larger and larger to the youngster and he disappears in his burrow.

Remember that prairie dog pictures alone will not round out your

Author and friend on a Dakota prairie. (Cecilia Costello)

photo sequence. Scenic views of the dog town and the mounds are part of the story; so are rabbits, antelopes, birds, and other associates. If you can photograph the prairie dogs in silhouette with back lighting just before sundown, you will have a picture to treasure.

138

Some people believe it is almost sundown for the prairie dog as a species in nature. Other authorities believe there is hope for them. In 1958 Ronald E. Smith reported that 2,442,955 acres of prairie dog towns in Kansas had been destroyed in fifty-two years. Less than 57,045 acres of towns remained, and 20,000 of these were to be destroyed in 1957. He predicted that in ten years the prairie dog in Kansas would be a "conversation piece," but his prediction has not yet come to pass. I found a few prairie dogs in Kansas in 1968 and learned that some farmers and ranchers are thinking of control, or suppression, of these animals rather than extermination.

E. Lendell Cockrum in his book, *The Recent Mammals of Arizona,* published in 1960, reported that the black-tailed prairie dog is now extinct in that state, and the Zuni prairie dog, formerly widely distributed in central and northeastern Arizona, is greatly reduced in numbers and range.

In Texas, when Clarence Cottam and Milton Caroline summarized facts from a 1965 survey, they found there were more than 300 prairie dog towns in at least sixty-six counties.

In Colorado, a few colonies of Gunnison's prairie dog still remain and there is evidence that they are increasing in small areas. The Utah prairie dog, never abundant, was reported in 1963 to exist in only nine towns. I have no more recent estimates of its numbers, but control personnel in Utah have been instructed not to disturb this species.

In Nebraska, North Dakota, South Dakota, and Montana, some game department members refuse to pinpoint their dog towns for the federal control crews. John Madson, in his article in *Audubon* about black-footed ferrets and prairie dogs, wrote that survival of both will depend on curtailing or halting current organized control efforts. "It is an ironic fact of political life that the Department of the Interior issues lists of endangered wildlife at the same time as it administers rodent and predator control programs," he stated.

On private lands, there exist a few enlightened ranchers who may be the prairie dogs' last and best friends. Some of them want no government poisoning on their properties. Others like to keep intact a part of our natural heritage of the prairie and its animals.

One rancher told me, "I'd rather have a few prairie dogs in the south forty than a rock from the moon in my front yard." Many people will agree with him. We can always go to the moon for more rocks. But once the prairie dogs are gone, a part of life we have never really understood will be gone forever.

Opposite: author looking at prairie dog country. White Water Point, here on Grand Mesa in western Colorado, is 10,000 feet in elevation. The desert in the Gunnison Valley in right center of the photograph is 5,000 feet. Gunnison's prairie dogs have been found throughout this elevational range.

Black-tailed prairie dog, Cynomys ludovicianus ludovicianus.

Prairie Dog Species and Subspecies

PRAIRIE DOGS belong to the order Rodentia, which includes gophers, mice, porcupines, and other rodents. Mammalogists place them in the squirrel family (Sciuridae) since they are closely related to marmots, ground squirrels, and chipmunks.

Prairie dogs, as we have seen, were not scientifically named until 1815, when George Ord called them Louisiana marmots, *Arctomys ludovicianus*. In 1817, Rafinesque gave them the now-accepted generic name *Cynomys*. With the publication of Baird's *Mammals of North America* in 1857, two species, the black-tailed and the white-tailed prairie dog, were recognized.

In 1916, N. Hollister listed two subgenera and seven subspecies of prairie dogs. More recently the classification and distribution of prairie dogs have been described by E. Raymond Hall and Keith R. Kelson, in *The Mammals of North America*, and by Gerrit S. Miller, Jr., and Remington Kellogg in *List of North American Recent Mammals*.

Cynomys ludovicianus ludovicianus—black-tailed prairie dog. Range: This subspecies originally was distributed throughout the Great Plains from Saskatchewan, Canada, to west-central Texas and from the Rocky Mountains to about longitude 97 degrees West in central Nebraska, Kansas,

143

White-tailed prairie dog, Cynomys leucurus.

and Oklahoma. Populations have been greatly reduced by poisoning in recent years.

Cynomys ludovicianus arizonensis—Arizona prairie dog. Range: Formerly in southeastern Arizona, southern and central New Mexico, southwestern Texas, and adjacent parts of Sonora and Chihuahua, Mexico. E. Lendell Cockrum in *The Recent Mammals of Arizona* reports that it is now extinct in that state.

Cynomys mexicanus—Mexican prairie dog. Range: Southeastern Coahuila and northern San Luis Potosi; north to Saltillo; south to Vanegas, Mexico. One half of the tail of this prairie dog is black, whereas only one third of the tail is tipped with black on the black-tailed and Arizona prairie dogs.

Cynomys leucurus—white-tailed prairie dog. Range: Mountainous parts of Montana, Wyoming, Utah, and Colorado. Colonies still exist in North Park, Colorado, and in northeastern Utah. Unremitting poison campaigns have virtually eradicated the white-tailed prairie dogs. These prairie dogs hibernate at high altitudes in winter. They have been observed at elevations of twelve thousand feet in the Rocky Mountains.

Cynomys parvidens—Utah prairie dog. Range: The western outpost of the genus. Always restricted to Utah; occurred in nine counties in 1935; never widespread or abundant; now rare. Poison experts now have been instructed not to disturb this species, which originally was found in Buckskin Valley, Iron County, Utah. Some mammalogists consider the Utah prairie dog to be a subspecies of the white-tailed prairie dog, *Cynomys leucurus*. The Utah prairie dogs are uniformly brown or reddish in color; the terminal half of the tail is white, and a spot of black appears above the eyes.

Cynomys gunnisoni gunnisoni—Gunnison's prairie dog. Range: Mountainous regions of central and central-southern Colorado and northern New Mexico. Extensive poison campaigns and sylvatic plague have nearly exterminated these prairie dogs, which formerly were abundant in South Park and the Gunnison Valley in Colorado and in the Jemez Mountains in New Mexico. The terminal half of the white-tipped tail of *C. gunnisoni* is marked with a gray center.

Cynomys gunnisoni zuniensis — Zuni prairie dog. Range: Formerly widely distributed in southeastern Utah, southwestern Colorado, northwestern and west-central New Mexico, and north-central Arizona. Now greatly reduced in numbers and range. This subspecies of Gunnison's is larger, has more pinkish cinnamon color, and is less buffy and blackish.

Bibliography

Adams, Arthur W. "Prairie dog investigations, 1963," *North Dakota State Game and Fish Department*, 1964.

Allan, Philip F., and Ben Osborn. "Tall grass defeats prairie dogs," *Soil Conservation,* 20:103-105, 113 (1954).

Anderson, Kenneth N. "Airborne lab fights plague," *Today's Health,* 38:40-41 (1960).

Anthony, Adam. "Behavior patterns in a laboratory colony of prairie dogs, *Cynomys ludovicianus,*" *Journal of Mammalogy,* 36:69-78 (1955).

————, "Seasonal reproductive cycle in the normal and experimentally treated male prairie dog, *Cynomys ludovicianus,*" *Journal of Morphology,* 93:331-370 (1953).

————, and D. Foreman. "Observations on the reproductive cycle of the black-tailed prairie dog (*Cynomys ludovicianus*)," *Physiological Zoology,* 24:242-248 (1951).

Bailey, Vernon. *A Biological Survey of North Dakota.* Washington, D.C.: U.S. Department of Agriculture, North American Fauna, No. 49 (1926).

————. *A Biological Survey of Texas.* Washington, D.C.: U.S. Department of Agriculture, North American Fauna, No. 25 (1905).

————. *Mammals of New Mexico.* Washington, D.C.: U.S. Department of Agriculture, North American Fauna, No. 53 (1931).

Bakko, Eugene B., and Larry N. Brown. "Breeding biology of the white-tailed prairie dog, *Cynomys leucurus,* in Wyoming," *Journal of Mammalogy,* 48:100-112 (1967).

147

Bell, W. B. "Cooperative campaigns for the control of ground squirrels, prairie dogs, and jack rabbits," *Yearbook of the United States Department of Agriculture,* 1917, pp. 225-233, Washington, D.C., 1918.

Blight, Robert. "Truth about prairie dogs," *Current Literature,* 37:75-76 (1904).

Bond, Richard M. "Range rodents and plant succession," *Transactions of the North American Wildlife Conference,* 10:229-234 (1945).

Bryant, Monroe D. "Phylogeny of Nearctic Sciuridae," *American Midland Naturalist,* 33:257-390 (1945).

Burnett, W. L., and S. C. McCampbell. "The Zuni prairie dog in Monte-zuma County, Colorado," *Colorado Agricultural College Circular* No. 49 (1926).

Cahalane, Victor H. "Badger-coyote 'partnerships,'" *Journal of Mammalogy,* 31:354-355 (1950).

Cary, M. *A Biological Survey of Colorado.* Washington, D.C.: U.S. Department of Agriculture, North American Fauna, No. 33 (1911).

Cates, E. C. "Notes concerning a captive prairie-dog," *Journal of Mammalogy,* 8:33-37 (1927).

Clapp, Kennedy N. "Prairie dogs," *National Park Service, Region Three Quarterly,* 3:21-25 (1941).

Clark, Tim W. "Ecological roles of prairie dogs," *Wyoming Range Management,* No. 261, Laramie (1968).

Cockrum, E. Lendell. *The Recent Mammals of Arizona: Their Taxonomy and Distribution.* Tucson, Ariz.: University of Arizona Press, 1960.

Costello, David F. "Natural revegetation of abandoned plowed land in the mixed prairie association of northeastern Colorado," *Ecology,* 25:312-326 (1944).

Cottam, Clarence, and Milton Caroline. "The black-tailed prairie dog in Texas," *Texas Journal of Science,* 17:294-302 (1965).

Coues, Elliott. *The Expeditions of Zebulon Montgomery Pike, 1805-1807.* New York: Francis P. Harper, 1895.

————. *History of the Expedition under the Command of Lewis and Clark.* New York: Francis P. Harper, 1893.

Dale, H. F. "Prairie dogs as pets," *Outdoor Nebraska,* 24:22 (1947).

Dano, Lee E. "Cottontail rabbit *(Sylvilagus auduboni baileyi)* populations in relation to the prairie dog *(Cynomys ludovicianus ludovicianus)* towns." M.S. thesis, Colorado A & M College, 1952.

Davis, Allen Hill, Jr. "Winter activity of the black-tailed prairie dog in North-Central Colorado." M. S. thesis, Colorado State University, August, 1966.

Davis, Gordon E. "Tularaemia, susceptibility of the white-tailed prairie dog, *Cynomys leucurus* Merriam," *United States Public Health Reports,* 50:731-732 (1955).

Dearden, Lyle C. "The gross anatomy of the viscera of the prairie dog," *Journal of Mammalogy,* 34:15-27 (1953).

D'Ostilio, D. O. "Nesting status and food of the golden eagle in northern Colorado." M.S. thesis, University of Colorado, 1954.

Ecke, Dean H., and Clifford W. Johnson. "Plague in Colorado," *Public Health Monographs,* 6:2-37 (1952).

——— and ———. "Sylvatic plague in Park County, Colorado," *Transactions of the North American Wildlife Conference,* 15:191-196 (1950).

Erpino, Michael J. "Copulatory behavior in the white-tailed prairie dog," *American Midland Naturalist,* 79:250-251 (1968).

Etkin, William (ed.). *Social Behavior and Organization among Vertebrates.* Chicago: University of Chicago Press, 1964.

Fichter, Edson. "Control of jack rabbits and prairie dogs on range lands," *Journal of Range Management,* 6:16-24 (1953).

Foreman, Darhl Lois. "The normal reproductive cycle of the female prairie dog and the effects of light," *Anatomical Record,* 142:391-405 (1962).

———. "Observations and experimental modifications on the reproductive cycle of the female prairie dog *(Cynomys ludovicianus)*." Ph.D. thesis, University of Chicago, 1955.

Foster, B. E. "Provision of prairie-dog to escape drowning when town is submerged," *Journal of Mammalogy,* 5:266-268 (1924).

Garst, Warren. "Technique for capturing young prairie dogs," *Journal of Wildlife Management,* 26:108 (1962).

Griffin, James B. "Eastern North American archaeology: a summary," *Science,* 156:175-191 (1967).

Hall, E. Raymond, and Keith R. Kelson. *The Mammals of North America.* New York: Ronald Press Company, 1959.

Hibbard, Claude W. "*Cynomys ludovicianus ludovicianus* from the Pleistocene of Kansas," *Journal of Mammalogy,* 18:517-518 (1937).

Himes, Duncan P. "Behavior in an incipient black-tailed prairie dog town." M.S. thesis, Colorado State University, August, 1966.

Hollister, N. *A Systematic Account of the Prairie Dogs.* Washington, D.C.: U.S. Department of Agriculture, North American Fauna, No. 40 (1916).

Jellison, W. L. "Notes on the fleas of the prairie dog, with descriptions of a new subspecies," *U.S. Public Health Reports,* 54:840-844 (1939).

————. "Siphonaptera: The genus *Oropsylla* in North America *(Citellus, Callospermophilus, Cynomys,* and *Marmota* parasitized)," *Journal of Parasitology,* 31:83-97 (1945).

Jillson, B. C. "Habits of the prairie dog," *American Naturalist,* 5:24-29 (1871).

Johnson, George Edwin. "Observations on young prairie-dogs *(Cynomys ludovicianus)* born in the laboratory," *Journal of Mammalogy,* 8:110-115 (1927).

Jones, J. Knox, Jr. "Distribution and Taxonomy of Mammals of Nebraska," *University of Kansas Publications* (Museum of Natural History) 16:1-356 (1964).

Kelso, Leon H. "Food habits of prairie dogs." Washington, D.C.: U.S. Department of Agriculture Circular No. 529 (1939).

King, John A. "Social behavior of prairie dogs," *Scientific American,* 201: 128-134 (1959).

————. "Social behavior, social organization, and population dynamics in a black-tailed prairie-dog town in the Black Hills of South Dakota," *Contributions from the Laboratory of Vertebrate Biology,* No. 67 (University of Michigan), 1955.

Klauber, Laurence M. *Rattlesnakes.* Berkeley, Cal.: University of California Press, 1956.

Koford, Carl B. "Prairie dogs, whitefaces, and blue grama," Wildlife Society Monograph No. 3 (December, 1958).

Lechleitner, Robert R., L. Kartman, M. I. Goldenberg, and B. W. Hudson. "An epizootic of plague in Gunninson's prairie dogs *(Cynomys gunnisoni)* in south-central Colorado," *Ecology,* 49:734-743 (1968).

Longhurst, William M. "Observations of the ecology of the Gunnison prairie dog in Colorado," *Journal of Mammalogy,* 25:24-36 (1944).

Madson, John. "Dark days in dogtown," *Audubon,* 70:32-43 (1968).

Malin, James C. *The Grassland of North America—Prolegomena to its History.* Gloucester, Mass.: Peter Smith, 1967.

McCulloch, C. Y. "Populations and range effects of rodents on the sand sagebrush grasslands of western Oklahoma," Ph.D. thesis, Oklahoma State University, 1959.

Merriam, C. Hart. "The prairie dog of the Great Plains," *Yearbook of the U.S. Department of Agriculture for 1901,* Washington, D.C., 1902.

Miller, Gerrit S., Jr., and Remington Kellogg. *List of North American Recent Mammals.* Washington, D.C.: United States National Museum Bulletin 205, 1955.

Nelson, E. W. *Wild Animals of North America.* Washington, D.C.: National Geographic Society, 1930.

Norris, J. J. "Effect of rodents, rabbits, and cattle on two vegetation types in semi-desert range land," New Mexico Agricultural Experiment Station Bulletin 353 (1950).

Osborn, Ben. "Prairie dogs in shinnery (Oak Scrub) savannah," *Ecology,* 23:110-115 (1942).

————, and Philip F. Allan. "Vegetation of an abandoned prairie-dog town in tall grass prairie," *Ecology,* 30:322-332 (1949).

Phillips, P. "The distribution of rodents in overgrazed and normal grasslands in central Oklahoma," *Ecology,* 17:673-679 (1936).

"Rattlesnakes and owls," *Time,* 59:77 (February 25, 1952).

Scheffer, Theodore H. "Ecological comparisons of the plains prairie-dog and the Zuni species," *Transactions of the Kansas Academy of Science,* 49:401-406 (1947).

————. "Study of a small prairie-dog town," *Transactions of the Kansas Academy of Science,* 40:391-395 (1938).

Seton, Ernest Thompson. *Lives of Game Animals.* Garden City, N.Y.: Doubleday, Doran & Company, 1929.

Shadle, Albert R., Winifred Bolton, Barbara Garona, and Darwin Farber. "The extrusive growth and attrition of the incisors in *Cynomys l. ludovicianus* (Ord)," *Anatomical Record,* 93:349-353 (1945).

Silver, J. "Badger activities in prairie-dog control," *Journal of Mammalogy,* 9:63 (1928).

Smith, Ronald E. "Natural history of the prairie dog in Kansas," University of Kansas, Museum of Natural History and State Biological Survey, Miscellaneous Publication No. 16, June, 1958; Miscellaneous Publication No. 49 (with addenda by Stephen R. Wylie), September, 1967.

Soper, J. Dewey. "Discovery, habitat and distribution of the black-tailed prairie-dog in western Canada," *Journal of Mammalogy*, 19:290-300 (1938).

————. "Further data on the black-tailed prairie-dog in western Canada," *Journal of Mammalogy*, 25:47-48 (1944).

Squire, Lorene. "Cutie, a prairie pet," *Nature Magazine*, 6:135-139 (1925).

Stockard, A. H. "Observations on reproduction in the white-tailed prairie dog *(Cynomys leucurus)*," *Journal of Mammalogy*, 10:209-212 (1929).

————. "Studies of the female reproductive system of the prairie dog *Cynomys leucurus:* I. Gross morphology," *Papers of Michigan Academy of Science, Arts, and Letters,* 20:725-735 (1935).

————. "Studies of the internal anatomy of the prairie dog, *Cynomys leucurus:* II. Normal cyclic phenomena of the ovarian follicles." *Papers of Michigan Academy of Science, Arts, and Letters,* 22:671-689 (1937).

Tate, G. H. H. "Albino prairie-dog," *Journal of Mammalogy,* 28:62 (1947).

Taylor, Walter P., and W. B. Davis. *The Mammals of Texas.* Texas Game, Fish and Oyster Commission, Bulletin No. 27 (1947).

————, and J. V. G. Loftfield. "Damage to range grasses by the Zuni prairie dog," *U.S. Department of Agriculture Bulletin* 1227:1-15 (1924).

Thorp, James. "Effects of certain animals that live in the soils," *Scientific Monthly,* 68:180-191 (1949).

Tileston, Jules V. "Comparison of a white-tailed prairie dog town with a black-tailed prairie dog town in North Central Colorado." M. S. thesis, Colorado State University, 1961.

————, and R. R. Lechleitner. "Some comparisons of the black-tailed and white-tailed prairie dogs in north-central Colorado," *American Midland Naturalist,* 75:292-316 (1966).

Vetterling, John M. "Endoparasites of the black-tailed prairie dog of Northern Colorado." M. S. thesis, Colorado State University, 1962.

Bibliography

Waring, George Houstoun. "Sounds of black-tailed, white-tailed, and Gunnison's prairie dogs." Ph.D. thesis, Colorado State University, 1966.

Wedel, Waldo R. *Prehistoric Man on the Great Plains.* Norman, Okla.: University of Oklahoma Press, 1961.

Whitehead, L. C. "Notes on prairie-dogs," *Journal of Mammalogy,* 8:58 (1927).

Wilcomb, Maxwell, Jr. "A study of prairie dog burrow systems and the ecology of their arthropod inhabitants in central Oklahoma." Ph.D. thesis, University of Oklahoma, 1954.

Wood, Albert Elmer. "Pleistocene prairie-dog from Frederick, Oklahoma," *Journal of Mammalogy,* 14:160 (1933).

Young, Stanley P. "Longevity and other data on a male and a female prairie dog kept as pets," *Journal of Mammalogy,* 25:317-319 (1944).

Index

Italic page numbers indicate illustrations.